D1248101

HOW TO THINK AND SWING
LIKE A GOLF CHAMPION

DICK MAYER

HOW TO THINK AND SWING LIKE A GOLF CHAMPION

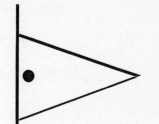

THOMAS Y. CROWELL COMPANY   NEW YORK

Copyright © 1958 by Dick Mayer

All rights reserved. No part of this book may
be reproduced in any form, except by a reviewer,
without the permission of the publisher.

Second Printing, March, 1958

Library of Congress Catalog Card No. 58-6837

Manufactured in the United States of America
by The Cornwall Press, Inc., Cornwall, N. Y.

Contents

PART III

PART IV

PART V

PART I

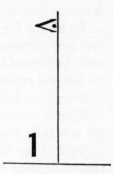

1

The New Way to Winning Golf

IN AUGUST of 1949 the lure of the fairways won out over the grind of business. For many years I had been thinking seriously of turning pro and now at last I decided to do so.

But it took four years of frustration, heartbreaks, and near misses before I won my first major tournament. In 1957 I finally won the tournament that all professional golfers dream about, the National Open. A few months later I won the richest tournament, the $50,000 Tam "World" and was also named "Golf's Man of the Year."

In those years I went from being just another also-ran on the tournament circuit to a winning golfer because of two things:

One, I developed a reliable golf swing, a swing that I could count on when the chips were down.

Two, I learned how to think out my game to prevent those errors that kept me from playing my best.

I had to learn both these things the hard way. As a 165-pounder, I'm not a particularly long ball hitter; therefore, accuracy became my chief objective.

To hit the big money I had to take my whole game apart, test new theories, experiment, reject, and try again. And most important of all, I had to learn to play the percentages on the golf course.

Everything I have learned will be in this book.

What I learned, you can learn too. And, profiting from my mistakes, you can learn *faster*.

None of my ideas are complicated. On the contrary, I've constantly tried to make my own game as simple as possible. For example, I play the ball from the same position on every shot except when circumstances require a "finesse" shot. I found that if I had to worry about placing the ball differently for different clubs, my game suffered.

In this book I've tried to make golf as uncomplicated as possible; to eliminate the unnecessary so that you can concentrate on the vital aspect of the game: winning.

We'll develop a step-by-step pathway to the goal of all golfers, breaking par. But first, we'll start with the 100-plus shooter.

2

The Basic Four Clubs

IN ANOTHER FIFTEEN YEARS we'll have an entirely new crop of golfers. Each year more and more youngsters are taking up the game. Moreover, they are getting better instruction and they are learning quicker and better.

Every parent, I believe, should encourage his youngsters to start golf. It is a healthful sport that can be played until we are very old and very gray indeed. Then, too, golf is becoming more and more a social aspect of our lives. Many business or professional men consider their game a business "asset."

Each year more and more adults are taking up golf. Some have never played at all before. Others are rediscovering the fun and relaxation of a friendly round on the links.

Fortunately age is no barrier to learning the game. I know one man who never touched a golf club until he was in his forties. Yet in a few years he became good enough to win his club championship. Every pro can cite similar experiences with their students.

Women in ever increasing numbers are playing golf. In many ways they can pick up the game more easily than men, because most women have a natural sense of timing and balance, essential elements of a good golf swing.

If you do not yet own a set of golf clubs, let me strongly urge you to let your pro help you pick out your set. His business is golf and he will guarantee you the right "fit." Buying cheap clubs is a poor investment. And choosing clubs which don't fit you and your game is like buying the wrong tools for a do-it-yourself project.

I believe every golfer should have a full set of matched clubs. One of the goals we are going to strive for is a reliable swing which will be suitable for every club in the bag. It stands to reason that you can accomplish this more easily if you start with a set of clubs that are matched.

What clubs should you carry as a beginner?

Everybody should carry a driver. This club, also known as the No. 1 wood, is designed to give you maximum distance off the tee.

I myself rarely carry a No. 2 wood (also called a brassie). This club is designed for long shots off the fairway. But it is only safe to use a No. 2 wood from a perfect lie and therefore I usually leave it out of my bag.

However, if you are having trouble getting height on your tee shots, the more lofted brassie may be the key to your driving problems.

A No. 3 wood, or spoon, is a very handy club. While it gives you a little less distance than a brassie, it has more loft. The club face is more slanted. This means a No. 3 wood makes it easier to get the ball into the air from the average fairway lie.

The No. 4 wood is to me one of the most useful clubs in

my bag. It has a little more loft than the spoon for bad fairway lies.

I do not use a No. 5 wood, primarily because the rules of the game limit us to fourteen clubs, and I have to make a choice. But I think a beginner should include a No. 5 wood in his bag.

Let me tell you the reason for this advice, so you can judge for yourself. Nearly all golfers have trouble with a No. 2 iron until they become quite proficient. It is a fine club, but difficult to master. You can get about the same results, distance-wise, with a No. 5 wood. Furthermore, a No. 5 wood has sufficient weight to give you *confidence* in your shot and also allows you to get the ball air-borne with less effort.

Whether you carry a No. 6 wood or a No. 3 iron is up to you. Again, I feel there is great merit to using a wood instead of an iron—for the same reasons which led me to recommend the No. 5 wood.

Eventually you should, of course, have a full set of irons running from No. 2 through 9. When your game improves sufficiently you will want to be in a position to choose which clubs you will carry on a given day, depending upon the weather, the condition of the particular course you are playing, and the way you are making your shots.

A wedge is one of the most valuable clubs in the bag *providing you are a good player*. There is a sand wedge for getting out of traps and a pitching wedge for short approach shots. I carry both, and I know you will want to also when we get your game to that stage. But, for now, I suggest that you leave both wedges out of your bag.

Finally, of course, you will carry a putter. There are a great many different kinds of putters on the market. Each has its advocates.

Personally I prefer the mallet-type putter. It has more weight than the blade-type, and I find it suits my style of putting best. Here again I think you should consult your

pro. He will probably recommend that you try out severa
until you find one which feels right for you.

Every club in your bag has a special purpose. Eventuall
you will master each of them. Unfortunately too many golf
ers have failed to master even one. I think the way to learn
how to use all your clubs is to start with a few and work only
with them until you know exactly what you can do with
each one.

So for a while let's limit ourselves to four clubs—a No.
wood, a No. 5 iron, a No. 8 iron, and a putter.

If you don't have a No. 4 wood, you can substitute a No
3 wood. But again let me strongly urge that you add a No.
wood to your set as soon as possible. With it you will be
able to handle both your driving and your long fairway shots

I picked the No. 5 iron because it is designed for medium
length shots. It is also a versatile club; you may use it for
short tee shots, for approaching, and for chipping.

The No. 8 iron is also a handyman club: for the short ap
proach shots, some chipping, and for getting out of tough
rough, and right now for sand traps. Later of course you'l
want to use a sand wedge.

And you'll need a putter.

Until you have *mastered* these four, you will have little
chance of mastering the other clubs in your bag. But once
you have mastered these four you will find it a simple task
to master the rest.

This four-club approach will provide several importan
side benefits. First off, you will gain confidence. This i
extremely important. When I won the Tam "World,"
Charles Bartlett, the very capable golf writer for the Chicago
Tribune, spotted my "secret."

"Mayer," he wrote, "knows how to bank on a single club
in tough spots. In this case it was a No. 4 wood."

Using only four clubs will also give you the benefit of an
other vital point of winning golf—the ability to judge dis

tance. Once you have mastered these four clubs you'll know just what distance you can expect from the No. 4 wood, 5 iron, and 8 iron.

Then, when you come to a problem shot, you'll know, for example, that the distance you need to make is just slightly more, or less, than your No. 5 iron. Then you will know that you've got to go down one club to the No. 4 iron, or up to a No. 6 iron.

You'll also learn one of the finer points of golf that will be vital when your score gets close to par. That is the ability to play the trick shots. But you aren't ready to try them yet.

Nevertheless it is obvious that if you have only four clubs to choose from and your No. 5 iron will carry your ball too far, then you'll have to take an easier swing so as not to overshoot your target. That, with a few refinements, is a favorite shot of the pros.

Now, quite clearly, you will not play as well with four clubs as you would with the full fourteen sticks in your bag. When I experimented with this idea some years ago, I found my score averaged about four strokes higher on eighteen holes. My score was higher only because I did not have the versatility to my game that is essential to a pro. Using only four clubs will also probably add a few strokes to your game *at first*. For example, your No. 5 iron may not quite carry you to the green; so you'll have to play short and safe.

But that is a good lesson too. Knowing when to gamble and when to play safe is one secret to top performance on a golf course. The four-club approach will start your lesson in that vital point of the game.

In a short while, maybe even from the first, you'll find that the four-club approach will *save* you strokes. But, most important, it will be giving you the foundation of the game you will need later on when you tackle the problem of licking par.

In the next chapter I'll have more to say about the four-club approach. But first I'd like to make one more important point.

As a newcomer to golf, you have a great advantage over many other golfers. You have no bad golf habits. Any golf instructor welcomes the chance to work with a beginner. He, or she, is easier to teach because no "built-in" errors must be corrected.

To capitalize on this advantage, the newcomer should spend a lot of time on fundamentals. There are only three: grip, stance, and swing. Yet all three are vital. Without all three you can never become a good golfer.

I don't expect you to work at your game as hard as I do. After all, golf is my business. Probably you can't spend long hours on the practice tee.

But I do believe you should devote fifteen or twenty minutes a day to working on these basic steps of golf. As a matter of fact, I'd rather see you spend a little time each day, than an hour once a week.

Why do I say this?

Well, because good golf is largely a matter of good golf habits. If you spend a little time each day, you will gradually make good golf habits *instinctive*.

At first you'll have to concentrate on each of these vital fundamentals. In a way golf is like learning to play the piano. At the start you have to watch the keys. But, with practice, you can soon forget your fingers and concentrate on the music.

In golf our goal is to build up your golfing habits so that every movement will become instinctive. After that you can concentrate on the job of playing winning golf.

3

How to Break 100

IF YOU HAVE played golf for a while and have not broken 100 consistently, there is one reason for your trouble. You are simply taking too many strokes.

Now I'm not just being funny when I say that. I have played in hundreds of pro-amateur tournaments and this experience has given me an opportunity to watch golfers of varying shades of skill.

The 100-plus shooter has *unnecessarily* thrown away vital strokes *that he didn't have to lose.* He has thrown away strokes by gambling on a shot he had to hit perfectly. Even a pro won't gamble on the perfect shot.

A second fault I have noted about the 100-plus shooter is that he has failed to master the fundamentals of the game. He has not learned how to use his clubs properly.

There is only one cure for this problem and it isn't an easy one. If you are in the 100-plus category, you've got to scrap your present game and rebuild a new one, just as I rebuilt mine.

As I say, this won't be easy because you already have some golf habits that have got you into trouble. Now you must unlearn them. You've probably got used to living with a bad slice. You are sure your grip is all right and, while your swing isn't quite what you'd like it to be, it's OK for your game.

Besides, you say, it isn't as if I'm a rank beginner just taking up the game. I'm out of the novice class.

Moreover, you may have already tried to make over your game. Then, when you went out on the course a few times and attempted to put those theories into practice, you wound up by shooting worse than ever.

I certainly understand this viewpoint. And furthermore, I must warn you that if you follow my advice, you'll probably add a few strokes to your game at first. Any time you experiment you're bound to have problems at the start. Your old habits will creep back into your game; the new method won't "feel right."

Now there are some "get-well-quick" teaching methods in golf. You can "cure" a certain number of golf faults mighty easily. A bad slice, for example, can be "corrected" by moving your hands around farther to the right on the grip and by taking an exaggerated closed stance.

Among the teaching pros this is known as the "aspirin-tablet" method. You've corrected one fault by adding another—an occasional bad hook. You get temporary relief—but that's all.

Yes, if you only want to break 100, you can probably do it by the "aspirin-tablet" method. But I am assuming that you really want to *improve* your game, not merely find temporary relief. That you have the ambition to shoot good golf; not merely develop a passable game.

If so, there's only one way you can do it. You've got to

go back to the beginner stage and learn the basic steps of grip, stance, and swing.

If you are shooting over 100 you've got to face the golfing realities of life. Actually you do *not* know and do *not* practice the correct fundamentals. Until you're willing to acknowledge this fact, you are dooming yourself to a life of so-so golf.

The decision to remake your golf game is not an easy one. But, once you have taken it, you will find that the task is not so hard after all. In the chapters ahead I will show you the correct grip, the proper stance, and the essentials of a smooth, reliable swing.

Just as I advised beginners in the last chapter, I urge you now to take a few minutes each day for practice. Regular practice periods will help ground you in the proper fundamentals and then your score will begin to show improvement.

I also recommend that you try the four-club approach. If you find it "embarrassing" to walk out on the course with only four clubs, take the rest along as well. But concentrate on the four: the No. 4 wood, No. 5 iron, No. 8 iron, and putter.

One other word of caution. Be patient. You aren't going to remake your game in a day. If you have bad golf habits, you've taken time to develop them. It will certainly take time to break them.

So don't rush out on the course bragging to your foursome about a new system that is going to make you into a par golfer overnight. Give the system a chance to work. If you do so, your score will be proof enough of your progress.

And above all, don't wait until the last moment before an important match to employ my system. I do my own experimenting on the practice tee or during a practice round. Sometimes, when my game is off, I'll even practice in a tournament. For example, the Tam Open comes a week before the "World," where the big money is. Because I had been playing poorly for a few weeks, I used the Open to sharpen up my game; then went on to win the Big One.

In this book I'll show you how to play your best game under pressure. But don't add to the pressure of an important match by experimenting just before you tee off. Ideally I think you should spend at least two weeks practicing fundamentals for fifteen to twenty minutes a day. Then if you put in enough time on the practice tee or driving range to gain confidence in your new swing, try it out on the course a few times.

By then your new golf habits will have started to take hold. But be sure you know these fundamentals. A hurried glance at a golf book won't teach them to you. You've got to drill them into your subconscious until they are automatic.

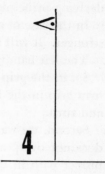

4

The Beginner's Biggest Error

A FRIEND OF MINE is the pro at one of the Midwest's finer country clubs. Recently we were discussing the problems of the amateur golfer.

"Nearly every golfer who shoots over 100 has a poor grip," my friend declared. "Even among the better players, probably half or more have an incorrect grip. But the trouble is that they won't recognize it.

"I try to tell them about fundamentals, but they say, 'Now don't tell me about the grip; I know all about it.'

"The trouble is that they don't, and they'll never improve until they do."

Now exactly what constitutes the right grip?

If you have the right grip the club will be firm in your hands throughout the swing. If you have the right grip the club head will return square to the ball. If you have the right grip the two hands will work together as a single unit for smoothness and power through the hitting area.

15

There are a number of variations to the grip, but the underlying principles remain the same.

In the case of a right-handed person, the right hand is the stronger. It will supply the power to your swing.

The left hand *guides* the swing.

So, in the grip we are looking for two things. We want a firm grip in the left hand so that the club head doesn't slip and turn.

Second, we want a grip in which the stronger right hand does not overpower the weaker left and *force* it out of its proper path in the arc of the swing.

Let's start first with the left hand. I believe that the club should be held primarily in the palm of the left hand. This enables you to get a firm, positive grip on the club.

There are two methods of gripping the club in the left hand. One is primarily with the fingers. The other is basically a palm and finger grip. Both systems have their followers.

However, I strongly recommend the grip in which the club is held in the *palm* and fingers of the left hand. This utilizes the full gripping power of the left hand and gives you much more firmness and confidence through the hitting area.

Here's how to form the proper grip with the left hand.

Place one of your clubs—an iron or a wood—on the ground so that it will be in the position to hit the ball squarely. Place your left palm, hand open, below the top of the shaft.

Turn your left palm so that the shaft lies along the first joint of the forefinger and up to the heel of the hand. Now, when you close your hand over the shaft, the grip will be below the fat part (the heel) of your hand.

To explain it another way:

Hold your left hand up in front of you. Make a fist. Now open your hand again. This time start to make a fist but keep your fingers stiff. Naturally you can only close it part way.

Notice there is a crease above your fingers which runs nearly across your entire hand. The shaft should run roughly across your hand and above that crease.

Now let's try it again with the club in the proper position on the ground. Fold your hand around the club. The thumb will fit down the shaft, slightly to the right of the shaft as you look down it.

You will notice that there is a V formed by the thumb and forefinger. This V should point toward the inside of the right shoulder.

The sensation you should feel in your left hand is that the club is being held in place by the fatty part (the heel) of your hand. Looking down at your left hand you should be able to see two knuckles, the knuckles of your forefinger and middle finger.

If you see three knuckles, your hand is too far around on the right. If you see only one, your hand is too far left.

In making each of these tests, make sure the club head is square to the target. It is very easy to "think" the V's are pointing correctly, when really you are only turning the club head.

Also, I recommend that you form your grip about a half inch down the shaft. In other words, don't grasp it at the very end. By gripping down the shaft a little way you get better control of the club.

Now, with only the left hand holding the club, swing it back and forth a few times, keeping the left arm straight. *Does it feel secure in your hand?*

If it slips at all, try again, paying particular attention to *a firmness in your little finger and the heel of the hand.* This is really the key area of grip for the left hand.

Let me issue an important warning right now, particularly to the 100-plus shooter. This grip is *not* going to feel comfortable at first. As a matter of fact, it will probably feel quite awkward. It did for me too, at first. In time, however, you will find it becoming the only natural way to hold a club.

Beginners should also remember that the golf grip is something new. Most men have played some baseball, and baseball depends on an entirely different set of muscles than you'll use in golf. So when you take up golf you've got to condition a brand-new set of muscles, particularly in the hands.

Once you feel you have the proper grip in the left hand, then add the right hand to the club. The right hand more or less "shakes hands" with the shaft of the club.

There are several ways of adding the right hand to the club. The original grip was a baseball grip. In this grip the right hand was placed below the left, with the shaft held in all fingers.

Chick Evans was the great master of this grip. It may feel "natural" to a beginning golfer. But it is extremely difficult to get a consistent swing with this grip because the right hand tends to dominate the left.

A second grip is the interlocking grip. Here the little finger of the right hand is hooked into the space between the forefinger and middle finger of the left hand.

Gene Sarazen, Lloyd Mangrum and Claude Harmon are among the name pros who use the interlocking grip. They feel it joins the two hands together, especially for golfers with small hands.

Yet by far and away the most popular grip is the Vardon overlapping. I use it and I believe every golfer should too. The fact that an overwhelming percentage of pros and top amateurs use the overlapping is, I think, the best proof that it is the most suitable and most effective grip of all.

Here the right hand is pressed up firmly against the left. It is the right little finger which does the "overlapping" from which the grip gets its name.

After you have your left hand properly on the shaft, bring your right hand up so that the right ring finger is flush against the left forefinger. The little finger then rests either on the back of the left forefinger or slightly behind it.

Personally I place the right little finger behind the right forefinger. This seems to give me a firmer grip and a greater awareness of the hands working together during my golf swing.

The thumb of the right hand is slightly to the left of the shaft as you look down.

As you recall, I emphasized that the grip of the left hand was primarily in the palm. The opposite is true of the right hand. Here the grip is primarily in the fingers.

If you grip too much with the palm of the right, it will tend to restrict the club head at the top of the backswing and "lock" your swing.

It is also vital that the V formed by the forefinger and thumb of the right hand should point toward the inside of your right shoulder, just as the V of the left hand did.

There are two common faults in grip. One is to point the V of the left hand toward the left shoulder and the V of the right hand toward the right; or vice versa. The second is to have the V of the left hand pointing upward, the V of the right slightly to the right.

In either case the hands are "fighting each other." They can't move together, act together as they must for a smooth, reliable swing.

Once you feel you have the grip formed properly, swing the club back and forth as you did with the left hand alone. Check to be sure that the club face is coming back square. Now I'm not talking about a long swing; just a foot or so back and a foot or so through where the ball would normally be lying.

One of the best checks I know for testing your grip is to stand in front of a full-length mirror. Pick up your club as you normally do; then check in the mirror to see if you are holding it so the V's are pointed properly.

Here's another trick I use regularly. Leave one of your clubs somewhere handy around the house, and occasionally check your grip.

As we progress in our golf, I'll remind you from time to time about your grip. Equally important, constantly remind yourself. Nearly every serious golf fault can be traced to an improper grip. The over-100 shooter can usually correct his faults by correcting his grip; the beginner can avoid future problems by learning the grip right from the start.

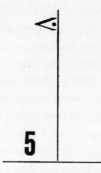

The "Tripod" Stance

"**S**TANCE" means the way you stand to the ball. Once you have found the proper way to grip the club, the next step is to learn how to address the ball properly.

Let's first discuss what our stance should do for us. Fundamentally, we want balance. We want to get a firm footing so that when we swing the club we'll have a solid base.

Then too we want a stance which will permit the hips and shoulders to turn freely. This is the basis for our power. We also want a stance that will enable us to hit strongly through the ball at impact.

For the time being put your clubs aside. I want to explain fully the details of the proper stance before we attempt to put it into practice with a golf club.

At address the knees should be flexed slightly, and the weight should be back on the heels. This is what pros frequently refer to as "sitting down" to the ball.

To illustrate this point, stand with your feet a little more than shoulder-width apart. Just stand naturally with your weight equally distributed between the right and left sides of your body.

Now flex your knees slightly. Actually what I mean is to "unlock" them. Get the feeling you can jiggle up and down. Also keep your weight back toward your heels. I don't mean to lean back, but to *feel* that your weight is more toward your heels than your toes.

The combination of flexed knees and weight somewhat back on the heels gives you a soiid feeling. You should feel confident that if someone suddenly tapped you from any side you wouldn't fall over.

In this position your feet are solid, but the flexed knees give you freedom to move.

Now hold your club in your hands, first forming the proper grip, and take your address with knees slightly bent, weight somewhat back. Feel that "sitting-down" sensation as you take your address.

Now simply swing the club back and forth a few feet on either side. Notice how your knees "give" with the swing, how your weight transfers smoothly from right to left and back again.

This "sitting-down" position prevents the common errors of falling into the ball, falling away, or swaying off line as you swing your club.

Now we have combined two points of the game: the proper grip and the correct "sitting-down" position.

There are three basic positions for your feet. If you imagine a line running through the ball and leading directly to your target, this would be the line of flight the ball would take if it went perfectly straight.

If your feet are set so that your toes are equally distant from the line of flight, you would be in a square position.

This is called a "square" stance and is used for the middle irons.

If your right foot is withdrawn farther from the line, your body will be turned slightly to the right. This is called a "closed" stance.

If, on the other hand, your left foot is farther back than your right from the line of flight, you will be facing slightly more toward your target. This is called an "open" stance.

Now, if you have been standing naturally, your toes are pointing slightly outward. For a great many years most instructors taught this toes-out position for the address to the ball. I used to play that way myself. But I found that I tended to sway on my backswing. I wanted a more stable stance, one which would eliminate this error-causing lateral movement.

I adopted a "tripod" stance.

In my opinion this is the only correct stance for every golfer, regardless of his height or weight. It assures proper footwork and balance.

Here's how I form my stance:

Stand with your *heels* about shoulder-width apart. Many persons have difficulty in judging the term "shoulder-width." One way to check is to get a wooden yardstick; have someone measure your shoulder width; then, placing the yardstick on the ground, place your heels the correct distance apart.

Your feet point perfectly straight toward our imaginary line of flight. Now turn the toe of your left shoe to the left about four inches. The distance I turn out my left foot is about the width of my shoe. In other words, the right foot is square, the left toe is pointing outward.

In a later chapter I'll go into some of the variations of this stance. But essentially the right foot in the square position becomes a brace preventing too big a turn by the hips and keeps the body from swaying to the right.

Now, with one more slight adjustment you'll have the correct stance for your No. 4 wood. With it we employ a slightly closed stance. To close your stance slightly, bring the right foot away about an inch from the line of flight.

Let's see how it looks when we combine all the points we have covered so far.

Place a ball on the ground.

(It may help visualize the imaginary line of flight if you set another club on the ground along this line of flight.)

Take the No. 4 wood in your left hand, forming the correct grip, and place the club head behind the ball, just as though you were about to start your swing.

Hold your left arm and the club shaft so they form a reasonably straight line.

Take your position with your left heel about two inches ahead of the ball (by ahead I mean closer to the target).

Now place your right foot about shoulder-width away from the left, and the toe of the right shoe about one inch farther away from the imaginary line of flight than the left toe. The right foot is square to the line of flight.

Now turn the toe of your left shoe out about four inches.

Next, grasp the club in the proper position with the right hand.

Flex the knees slightly to achieve that "sitting-down" feeling.

In this position you should feel that your weight is evenly balanced, but that in your right side the weight is on the instep of your foot. There is a certain amount of pressure on the inside of the right thigh.

The knees too should feel as if they are pushing toward each other.

Now I've gone into a lengthy discussion about the tripod stance primarily because it takes a lot of words to describe these separate movements so that there will be no misunderstanding.

Actually, after years of playing I take my stance without a

single conscious thought. I just stand so that I feel comfortable, line up my target, and swing. So will you after you have practiced enough for the grip and stance to become instinctive.

To practice your stance, follow this pattern.

First work for a while on the fundamentals of the stance. When you think you have it down pat, take the second step.

Place the ball on the ground.

Place the club head back of the ball.

Now, glancing at your target, take your proper stance. As you make this movement, raise the club head high enough so it won't accidentally strike the ball.

Then when you are all set, replace the club head back of the ball.

(This, as you will learn shortly, is exactly the way I get set and the way most pros take their stance.)

In your practice, recheck each of the fundamentals. Is the club head square? Is your stance slightly closed? Is your weight back on your heels with a sitting-down feeling? Is the weight on your right side centered on the right instep and along the inside of your right leg?

Are you in perfect balance?

I want you to spend plenty of time on the grip and stance before you go on to the next chapter.

There is a very sound reason for this.

If you try to swing at a golf ball while you are worrying about your hands, your feet, your weight, and a dozen other things, you won't have your mind free for the essential business at hand—hitting the golf ball where you want it to go.

To push ahead before your grip and stance become *instinctive* is a good deal like trying to enter college right after your freshman year in high school. You aren't ready yet.

Let me re-emphasize that point.

Unless you have practiced your grip and stance until it becomes automatic and you no longer have to think about it, you are only inviting confusion and trouble. Once you start learning to put your swing in motion, you'll have other things to think about. You may find yourself wasting a lot of time just searching for the answer to some golf fault you would never have acquired if you had been more patient in these early stages of learning good golf.

You'll note that chapter 10 covers "curing your faults." There would be little need for such a chapter if every golfer would take time really to learn the fundamentals. I know from experience, however, that a great many people won't listen to this warning. They try to rush their game ahead too fast.

So I must repeat: If you wish to be able to skip that chapter (and avoid weeks of playing with *no* improvement in your score), take it easy now. In the long run you'll be ahead both in time and in golfing skill.

Now that we've discussed the No. 4 wood stance, let's take up the second of the four clubs on which we are going to build our game. The stance for the No. 5 iron is precisely the same except for two simple changes.

Instead of the slightly closed stance, we will use a square stance now. This, you recall, means that the toes of both feet will be an equal distance from our imaginary line of flight.

Secondly, the heels will be closer together. Instead of shoulder width, as they were with the No. 4 wood, they will be about three-fourths that distance apart. Again, remember your right foot is square, the left foot pointed outward.

With our third club, the No. 8 iron, our stance will be slightly open, the left foot drawn back about an inch from the line of flight. With this club our heels will be closer together, roughly half the width we used with a No. 4 wood.

Later, when we add the other clubs to your game, you will find that the same rule of stance applies. You gradually narrow your stance as you progress to the shorter and shorter clubs.

All right.

Now I want you to put a book marker at this page and after you read the closing paragraphs of this chapter, put the book down and practice the points we have discussed.

And, don't reopen it until you have *mastered* them. By mastering them I don't mean trying each just a few times. I mean practicing them until you have them down pat; until they become as natural and instinctive as tying your shoelaces or knotting your tie.

Put a ball down on the ground and take your proper stance with your No. 4 wood. Put it aside and try your No. 5 iron. Next, your No. 8 iron.

Take it slow at first, always remembering that your grip is of primary importance. Next, the position of your feet. Third, your proper balance.

In a short time (but don't rush it), you'll find yourself always gripping the club properly and you can eliminate this check point. Next, you'll find you always put your feet in the right position. Then you can forget that.

And somewhat later, you'll find you automatically assume the proper balance.

When you've reached that point you are well on your way to playing expert golf, *even though you have not yet swung a club*. That is how important these early lessons are.

Two final reminders before I leave you to your practicing. First, with every club we'll play the ball in the same position —about two inches to the right of the left heel. Always address a ball when practicing these fundamentals because doing so helps you visualize the shot better.

The second point I deliberately skipped up to now because you've already learned it. Nevertheless some beginners always want to know how far away from the ball they should stand. Actually if you stand with your weight properly back toward your heels and your hands hang naturally, you will be standing at the proper distance from the ball. For most golfers the hands are just slightly in front of the body.

The major error to avoid is reaching out for the ball and getting your weight forward on the balls of your feet.

If you've really followed our lessons so far you are addressing the ball properly.

So, close the book and practice until you are sure that both grip and stance are an instinctive part of your developing golf game.

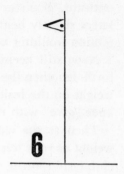

6

Grooving Your Swing

Now, assuming that you have taken time to learn the prinicples of proper grip and stance, we are ready to put your swing into action. If the initial steps have become instinctive, you will have no trouble in putting your swing to work.

Take your No. 4 wood and position it on the ground with the correct grip and stance. We won't use a ball yet in this exercise. After you've assumed your stance, take the club back about two feet keeping the wrists firm.

Just swing the club back and forth with your wrists firm. Keep your knees firm.

After you've swung the club back and forth a half dozen times without stopping, keep the club swinging, but now let your left knee "give" with the swing.

Be sure that the weight of the right foot is on the inside spikes of your golf shoes.

Note what happens to your left knee. As it "gives" with

your left-to-right swing, it moves to the right and slightly outward. You see, don't you, the importance of having *both* knees slightly bent? If either is stiff this naturally flowing motion wouldn't be possible.

Now, still keeping the club moving in its arc back and forth, lengthen the swing another foot, still maintaining your weight on the inside of your right foot and letting your left knee "give" with the swing.

Then as the club moves to the right, you can feel the weight of your left side on the instep of the *left* foot. As the club head returns, the weight in your left side seems to move to the outside of your left foot.

What is happening is simply this: the motion of the club head is making you shift your weight toward the direction in which the club head is moving.

Now, instead of swinging the club head back and forth, I want you to position your club and take your proper grip and stance. Still keeping your wrists firm, draw the club back about two feet. Don't drag it back slowly or jerk it back fast.

But *draw* it back, letting your left knee move at the same time.

After you've drawn the club back two feet or so, stop. Return the club back of the ball. Do this four or five times.

Next, do the same exercise, only carry the club head back about *three* feet. Repeat this four or five times.

By now you should be getting the feeling that the movement of the left knee (and that weight shift you can feel in your left foot) goes together with the backward movement of the club head.

What you are really experiencing is the first movement of your backswing. Some people feel that they start the club head back by a little "push" with their left instep. Still others feel the start in their hands.

Whatever feeling seems clearest to you is the right one for you—the "signal" that you've started your swing.

The important thing is that your hands have moved away together and that you've simultaneously started the weight shift from your left foot.

This is what the experts call a "one-piece" swing. It means that your hands and body are acting together, the formula for a smooth, reliable swing.

All right, let's try it again. Position your club. Draw your club back, this time almost to waist height. Note now what happens to your left foot. The weight is almost completely in your left instep.

At this point I want to emphasize a most important thing about your swing.

Your weight should be on your left instep and your right instep. Your left foot will *roll* over onto your instep.

Keep your left heel on the ground, or as close to the ground as you comfortably can.

Let me tell you why I emphasize the position of your left heel. If you let it get off the ground at this stage of the swing, the action of the heel will be exaggerated with a full swing. This can become a serious error, particularly among women golfers. They tend to swing the left heel outward at the top of the backswing and then fail to get it back into proper place on the downswing.

In golf it is almost axiomatic that one error can be corrected only by making a second. Pretty soon faults start doubling up, and you have a game filled with errors. Then only with pure luck can you ever expect to hit a golf ball squarely where you want it to go. Let us repeat then: the position of the left heel is not important by itself. It is, however, a handy check to see that you are taking the club away properly. Once you have determined that you always keep that left heel on the ground, or as close to the ground as possible, forget it.

This phase of your pivot will now become another of your golf instincts, and you will have one worry less.

I want you to note something else about your position when you have drawn the club head back about waist high.

Your hips now are turned about a quarter of the way. If you looked down at this point you would see the outside of your right toe. All right, you've passed another milestone— you've pivoted your hips properly. It isn't necessary to go into a detailed discussion of the matter now, but this correct hip action is a by-product of the tripod stance, which restricts the hip turn so that you keep in perfect balance throughout.

The other thing we've been stressing—drawing the club back smoothly—is also an important ingredient of a good golf swing. Some golfers drag the club back so slowly that they never get the "coiled-up" feeling at the top of the backswing which is a major source of power.

They have read somewhere that they should take the club head back slowly, and they've translated this advice into an almost painful, deliberate movement. In reality the backswing should be free and easy.

On the other hand you shouldn't swing the club head back too fast, either. For if you do it will be almost impossible to control both the club head and your own body during the backswing and the subsequent downswing.

A smooth-flowing backswing is the ideal to strive for. It is a little hard to tell you just how fast it should be. However, my own backswing is about two-thirds as fast as my downswing.

My backswing sets the tempo for my entire swing. When I want extra distance, I step up the entire tempo of my swing. So, keep a little reserve for those special occasions when you need extra yardage.

Now let's add one other factor to our lesson.

Instead of standing so that you look directly down at the ball, cock your chin slightly to the right.

And, most important, *keep your eye on the ball.*

I have noticed that amateurs tend to watch the club head as it moves back. This either causes them to "lean" to the right as the club head moves back, or forces them to snap their head back on the downswing to concentrate again on their target. By keeping your eye on the ball you will avoid making either mistake.

Keep practicing that initial movement of taking the club head back to about waist height, keeping your eye on the ball, and concentrating on a smooth backswing.

Most errors in the swing among beginners and 100-plus shooters occur in the first five feet of the backswing. If you've followed our lessons, however, you will have avoided common faults, like "picking up" the club with your hands instead of swinging the club head back smoothly and low to the ground.

Now as you get the club up about waist high with your hands firm, you will note that's about as far as you can go. To carry it farther, you must continue to pivot your shoulders and cock your wrists to complete your backswing.

Don't hurry your backswing in this exercise. Just take the club head back as far as you can and stop. Then start over again. Now let's take time out here to recheck two points: Is that left heel on or near the ground? Is your weight on the inside spikes of your right foot and, at the top of your backswing, on the inside spikes of your left?

Let's add a fourth check point—your grip.

At the top of your backswing, your grip—particularly your left hand—should be firm on the club.

Don't worry right now how far you take the club back at the top of your backswing. Too many golfers have watched the pros and think that in order to get distance they've got to take the club back far enough so that it is parallel or below parallel to the ground.

This is partly true. The bigger the arc of the swing, the

greater the distance *if you are a top player*. But a big arc in the hands of an inexperienced player will only cause trouble unless, and until, you can control your swing.

So, if a three-quarter swing is all you can manage safely, settle for that now. As you limber up your golf muscles, your swing will start to lengthen out.

But for now—and even when you become a par shooter— control of your swing is always the most important thing to strive for. *Distance—for the pro or the beginner—is far less important than accuracy.*

Unfortunately too many golfers "complete" their back-swing by letting go of the club with their left hand. The check point here is *the little finger of your left hand. It should be securely on the shaft at the top of your backswing.*

It is easy to prove this point. Take your club head to the top of your swing. Now loosen the little finger of your left hand. Notice how the club head drops a good six or eight inches. Now retighten that finger. Note how the club flies up.

That upward movement takes place every time you have an insecure left hand on your club. You complete your back-swing by loosening your grip. Then, as you start your down-swing, your first action is to retighten your grip.

This sets the club head in motion *in your hands.*

As a consequence, your hands have made their move and your wrists have uncocked while your downswing is only just starting. We call that "throwing" the club head or a "fly-casting" swing. Either way, you've lost power and accuracy.

One other check point in your backswing is the position of your right elbow. It should be pointing down to the ground at the top of your swing.

I myself have one fault I'm constantly fighting. If I'm not careful, my right elbow will start flying out on my back-swing and pretty soon I'm shooting all over the course. I have to watch this fault as much today as I did when I first became a pro.

To combat this flying right elbow, I have devised two exercises which I do regularly.

I have an elastic belt which I fasten around the muscle of my upper right arm and around my body. This "ties" my right arm to my side. The elastic in the belt has enough "give" so as not to restrict my swing.

Then, with my right arm fastened to my side, I take my practice swings.

I don't know of a better test to make sure you are keeping that right arm in close. Now, understand, in the correct swing the right arm isn't going to stay *pinned* to your side. It is going to stay reasonably close and with the elbow pointing downward.

Another good test is to put a handkerchief under your right armpit and see if you can swing without the handkerchief falling out. I have used—and will continue to use—both tests myself from time to time as a check against a flying right elbow.

Now that we've discussed the backswing in detail, let's work on the downswing.

All right. Take your position at the top of your backswing. Then, without moving your hands or arms, turn your hips back square as they were at the address.

Note what happens. Your shoulders move, your hands drop, and your weight moves back toward your left side again.

Try it once more. A third time.

This is the correct way to start the downswing. In my case, I feel that my left hip and left arm *initiate* the downswing. Perhaps you feel the start in your left knee. Or maybe in the shift of weight in your left foot.

The important thing is to feel that your left side initiates

the downswing. Whatever sensation translates that idea to
your subconscious is the one to concentrate upon.

All through this first movement your wrists should remain
cocked.

By the time your hips are square, your hands are down
about waist high. Now, as you recall, this was the point of
the backswing where the hands cocked.

On the downswing, this is the point for the hands to uncock—to pour the power of your wrists and hands through
the hitting area. I get the feeling that I'm trying to get my
left side out of the way as soon as possible on the downswing
and my hands delay their uncocking as long as possible.

Now let's put the whole swing together. As you hit
through the ball just let the club head travel its course.
Don't worry about the follow-through. If you've done everything right up to this point, you'll have a smooth follow-
through.

There is another action which will take place *automatically*. As you hit through the ball, you should also *keep your
eye on the spot where the ball was*. The natural movement
of the follow-through will pull your head up at the right
time. So, don't strain to keep your head in place after it
comes up naturally. On the other hand, don't look up too
soon or a topped shot will result.

Let me give a warning. You've heard, or read, a lot about
"pausing" at the top of your backswing. Well, forget it. I
don't think the swing should ever have any stopping point.
The concept of a "pause" is bad. If you stopped, you'd have
to start again. There's only one reason to stop and that is to
correct some error—to regrip the club or readjust. If you've
followed our step-by-step lessons, you haven't any reason to
pause at the top of your backswing.

Actually I can't stop my swing at the top. If you fired a
gun at the precise moment when I've reached the top of my

backswing, my club head would have moved down about six inches before I could consciously stop it.

So, rather than a pause, concentrate on the key point—a smooth backswing and a smooth downswing.

All right then, let's review the ingredients of the complete swing. Keep your weight balanced. Move smoothly through your swing. Save your hand action until you have moved your left side out of the way of your swing.

Now let's take the swing as a whole and note the various check points as we go.

1. Take your address. Check proper grip and stance.

2. Swing the club head back smoothly, letting the hips and weight shift move the club.

3. Complete your swing with the shoulder turn and cocking of the wrists. Check your left heel, right elbow.

4. The left side now initiates the downswing.

5. Delay the hand action until your hands have reached the hitting area.

Now I want you to keep swinging that golf club, making the checks I have suggested from time to time. Then, gradually eliminate the check points one by one. When you can forget them all, you will be started on the road to good golf.

Strive for rhythm and tempo. Don't rush your swing. Don't try to murder the ball. The rhythm and power of a well-coordinated swing will give you all the distance you need.

The swing with the No. 5 iron follows the same sequence. But since your stance will be narrower, the arc will be smaller.

The same sequence applies as well to the No. 8 iron, except that here you will normally use only a three-quarter or half swing. With this club, there is almost no body action. By this I mean your pivot is very limited and most of the swing comes from the arms and hands.

As with the No. 4 wood, make sure the blade of your No. 5 iron and No. 8 iron returns squarely to the ball. You will normally use these irons on shorter shots where accuracy is at a premium, so don't overswing.

Before we go out to the golf course, let me tell you about the weighted club. I carry one with me in the car wherever I go, and I always have one around the house.

Any time I have a few spare minutes I swing this club to keep my swing in shape.

The weighted club is simply a driver which has been built up with lead. My regular driver is 14⅛ ounces. I took one from the factory and fixed it up so that now it weighs about 24 ounces. In one sense the golfer with a weighted club is much like the baseball player who swings a leaded bat before he goes to the plate. However, as you will learn later in this book, it should never be used just before a regular match. This practice club helps loosen you up. But it has many other advantages.

For one thing, as we have already said, the average player hasn't developed *golf muscles*. Take Ellsworth Vines, for example. He was a championship tennis player, but when he turned to pro golf he had to build an entire new set of muscles.

I don't advocate squeezing balls or lifting weights or any of those other exercises used by some people to strengthen their wrists. I think the weighted club is the answer. With the weighted club you will be actually swinging a golf club. A heavy practice club makes you use the muscles that you are going to use in your regular golf swing.

Also, its extra weight helps you develop an arc to your swing. If you have faults, they'll show up more clearly with a weighted club and then you'll find it easier to correct them.

You can make your own weighted club if you care to. Remove the plate from the bottom of an old wood. Bore a number of holes in the wood and fill them with lead, making sure that the weight is always centered.

You must also be certain that the club has good strong wrappings; otherwise the added weight will cause the neck to crack. You must realize too that it takes a good deal of lead to build up the club weight, so figure on this in advance.

The easiest, and probably the best solution, is to buy a weighted club. There are also weighted head covers on the market which you can attach to your regular clubs.

Whether you make your own weighted club or buy one, I can't recommend this practice club too strongly. There are some made especially for women, too.

I wouldn't be without my weighted club. Of course, I never carry it out on the course in a tournament, yet in many ways the weighted club is the most valuable stick in my bag.

A few minutes a day with the heavy club is good exercise, winter or summer. Then, after practicing with it diligently, you'll soon find you'll hit 'em farther and you'll hit 'em better with your regular-weight clubs.

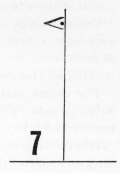

7

Developing Good Golf Habits

I DON'T EXPECT for one minute that you are ready to go right out on the course and break par. Not yet. You'll need time and experience to get your game down to that score.

Whether you're a beginner or a 100-plus shooter who is "remaking" his game, you are bound to muff your percentage of shots. You may whiff a few; dig your irons into the ground; slice your drives and dribble a few fairway shots just a few yards down the fairway.

That's to be expected at this point in your development. Still, if you'll keep at the fundamentals we have discussed so far, those faults will gradually disappear as you groove your swing and it becomes a smooth, reliable movement.

But it is not too early to start learning some of the professional's golf habits. You should develop a routine for every shot—*and stick to it.* Then it too will become part of your *instinctive* golf game.

First of all, *always take a practice swing before every shot.*
For one thing, this gives you a little time to get your
thoughts together. Also, in walking to your ball, certain muscles have been relaxed because your hands are hanging at
your sides.

The practice swing helps to loosen you up. Chances are
you will rarely use the same club twice in a row on an average round. And if, for example, you are switching from
your No. 4 wood to a No. 5 iron, that's quite a difference.
The practice swing helps you make the adjustment from club
to club.

Now I don't think you should take four or five practice
swings. That's too much. Normally just one will give you
good coordination. If it doesn't feel right, take another.

Most of the better pros take a practice swing. Cary Middlecoff, for example, takes little short swings walking up from
behind the ball, just to loosen up his muscles. I don't always take a full practice swing myself; sometimes I just ma-
nipulate the club in my hands.

But, for the average player, a regular practice swing before every wood or iron shot is essential.

If you start now, that practice swing will become a built-in
part of your game.

Here is the routine followed by the top pros:

1. They study the situation.
2. They take a practice swing.
3. They address the ball and hit it.

Let's put this routine into your game. You walk up to the
first tee. We'll assume you've taken a proper warm-up period
ahead of time.

Tee up your ball.

Then, standing about a yard or so in back of your ball,
take a practice swing with your driver.

*Take your practice swing always in the direction in which
you are going.* This applies to every practice swing on the

course. Always do it behind your ball and in the direction you are aiming.

In this way your practice swing is as close as possible to the shot you plan to play.

Let's say your drive goes out 180 yards and your next shot is coming up. As you walk up to where the ball landed, study the situation. How much distance do you need now? What are the problems ahead? If you aren't sure of the distance walk up ahead of your ball until you can see the green clearly and can judge how long a shot you have left.

Make your decision and *stick to it.*

Now walk around behind your ball and take your practice swing. Try to visualize where the ball would have gone if you had actually hit it with your practice swing, and make any necessary correction.

If there is any doubt in your mind as to whether you've selected the right club, settle it with your practice swing. That's the time to change your mind. If you're still in doubt when you swing at the ball, you're likely to flub the shot.

Since we're starting out with only four clubs—No. 4 wood, No. 5 iron, No. 8 iron, and putter—we won't be trying any finesse shots. We will concentrate on keeping the ball in play and worry about distance and pinpoint accuracy later.

However I can't stress too strongly the fact that you should *learn as you play.* How far are you hitting that No. 5 iron with a full shot? When you have a shot later on that is the distance you've hit your No. 5 iron, you'll *know* it's the right club.

Surprisingly enough that very simple observation has escaped thousands of amateur golfers. They have only the vaguest notion of what they can do with their different clubs. So if you can learn *club judgment* now you will be ahead of most golfers playing today.

Whenever the remaining distance to the green is less than your full No. 5 iron, cut down your swing. Again, keep learning. Learn exactly what you can do with that No. 5 iron. It is one of the most versatile clubs in your bag.

Another important aid to good golf is knowing how to tee up a ball properly. This is a good time to learn the way to do it.

At just about the middle of the club face is a "sweet spot" which gives you maximum distance and accuracy. Tee up the ball so that the club face will strike it on the "sweet spot."

You should tee up the ball on *every* tee shot.

Some golfers hit the ball off the ground, particularly on short par-3 holes. That's not very smart because a tee gives you the advantage of a "perfect" lie.

In teeing up the ball for a No. 8 iron, here's a general rule. There is a knob on the top of the tee which holds the ball. Just about that knob, or perhaps slightly more, should be sticking out of the ground.

With a No. 5 iron, tee up the ball just a trifle higher. For the No. 4 wood tee it up about the equivalent of a finger's width. If you tee too high, you'll "sky" the ball.

Now, let's discuss another "professional" phase of the game —the waggle. Some instructors believe the waggle is something that should not be taught until a golfer becomes experienced. I don't agree. I believe every golfer must waggle the club in one fashion or another.

The waggle is rhythmic, for one thing. It helps get the swing *in motion*. The waggle loosens up tension. It helps you get set for your shot.

There is only one way to waggle a club—and you've already learned how earlier in this book when we were discussing stance. You will recall that I told you to walk up to your ball, set your club face back of it, and raise the club face above the ball. Then, with your eyes on your target, set your feet, and waggle.

Now every golfer waggles a bit differently. But every good

player uses the waggle to loosen up, adjust his feet, and get his swing in motion.

My own particular mannerism is to place the club behind the ball, set my feet while swinging the club back and forth about a foot or so, then returning the club behind the ball and after that I'm set to go.

Some golfers will swing the club back and forth once, others several times. You should select the number of waggles which seems to "loosen" you up for your swing. Remember it is very important that the waggle should be in the same path the club head will later follow on your backswing.

Many golfers, including some tournament players, share a very common fault. They pay too much attention to their feet while addressing the ball. They glance at the hole and find out where they have to go. Next they set their feet and the blade of the club. Then they swing.

But when they do this many times they are not on the target. They are paying too much attention to details and not enough about where they must hit the ball.

If I followed their example I'd be off my target one way or the other, usually to the right.

Instead I walk up to the ball, set my club, start my waggle, and set my feet, one by one, and get my hands ready. *All the time I am looking at my target,* only occasionally glancing at the ball.

Your first job when you reach your ball is to decide the right distance between you and your target and pick out the right club and take your practice swing. At the same time you are also picking out your line of flight.

But you can't worry about the position of your feet or your grip, then suddenly look up and find you are off to the right, or left, of your objective.

The only time I look at the ball is to make sure the club doesn't accidentally hit the ball at address.

Now this isn't an easy lesson to learn, and it will take time.

But as you progress and hit enough golf balls, you will learn to look at the target and regulate everything else accordingly. You will learn to set yourself automatically.

You can pick up a cigarette or a glass by your side without looking at it, providing you know where it is. The same thing is true in golf. You don't have to look at the ball to know where it is.

Now I myself have made this mistake more than once; I've swung the club head away, knowing full well that I'd have to make some adjustment in my swing because I was aiming too far to the right of my target.

And there are times when you just can't seem to get set right and you'll miss a shot. We all do.

But the best system is to glance at your target and let your hands and feet set themselves according to memory and feel, and according to what you are seeing as you look at the target.

As I said before, you'll make errors. We all do. But by learning right now the proper golf habits, including a good waggle, you will be getting ready for par golf that much sooner.

As we have already explained, our goal with our four-club method is to keep the ball on the fairway so we are always moving toward the hole. Any time I hit every single fairway, I'm off to a sub-par round. But of course, I don't stay on the fairway every day; nor will you.

The rough is a place to avoid wasting shots. Always pick the club that you are *sure* will get you back on the fairway. If in doubt, take your No. 8 iron and just pitch the ball a few yards in a safe direction.

Concentrate on *keeping the ball in play*. If you do that, your score will automatically improve because you'll stop throwing away those needless strokes trying to do the impossible.

Finally, as you get close to the green, you'll want to use a chip shot. With a No. 5 iron and a No. 8 iron you have two of the handiest chipping clubs in the bag.

When you chip, the body should be completely still.

Chipping and putting are two highly individualistic phases of golf. In time nearly everyone develops his own technique for these two shots. When you find a method for chipping and putting that works for you, stick to it by all means. In your short game it is results that count. And if you are to score well you must be a good chipper and putter.

As you get within 130 yards of the green you are within the area of approaching and putting. An approach can be played with a No. 7 iron, No. 8 iron, or No. 9 iron, depending on the type of shot you decide upon.

At the present time I suggest that you aim those approach shots for the center of the green, rather than for the flag. By doing this you'll have a bigger target and less chance for error.

When you finally get in close—say 10 or 15 yards from the green—you are in the chipping area. A chip plainly enough doesn't have to travel very far to reach the green. A short, crisp stroke is the secret.

While there are differing techniques for this shot, nearly all pros will grip down on the club. By this I mean they will put their hands down an inch to four inches below their normal grip. This shortens the stroke and gives a firmer shot at the ball.

Your backswing should be short for chip shots; the club head should rarely go back more than halfway between the ground and waist high.

Some pros chip with almost nothing but hand action. Their arms move very little. They take the club back by cocking their wrists, using a minimum of arm movement. On their downswing they are careful to uncock their wrists and let the hands do the work.

Using this method, the pro will let the arms move on the

follow through to keep the club head close to the ground after it strikes the ball.

Another method favored by some pros is to move the arms back about a foot or a foot and a half and cock the wrists quickly. Again, the pro tries to keep the club head low to the ground after impact.

Still another method is to employ the same swing that you use with a regular shot, except that you don't take the club back as far. The wrists are kept fairly firm throughout the entire swing, relying on the length of the backswing and tempo of the swing to carry the ball the proper distance.

My own chips are a combination of shoulder and hand action. If I have a long shot, the shoulders will play a part. But for any short chip—25 or 30 feet—I depend mostly upon the arms and cock the wrists only slightly.

My advice is to try all three methods to find out which one works best for you. Generally speaking my method suits most golfers because there is less chance of the hands "giving" at impact and throwing the shot off-line.

The important thing about the chip shot is to keep your body completely still and your weight mostly on your left side. Your body provides the firm foundation for the arms and hands to swing the club head, and any movement of your body will throw the shot off-line. Because the ball is traveling such a short distance, even a small error in hitting it along the right line of flight may be costly.

There are several basic rules to follow in chipping:

Always line up the club head so that the ball will be struck squarely.

Take the club head back on the line of flight and follow through, keeping the club head along that path.

Above all, take your time. This is good advice on every shot, but especially on the short approach and chip. Easy does it.

Most people will start chipping badly when they take the

club away too fast. Because this is such a short shot, you unconsciously hurry it.

There is another common error in chipping. I've been guilty of it myself many times. After you get set, you change your mind. Either you think you should hit the ball harder, or you suddenly decide that the stroke you had in mind will carry your ball too far. As a result, you'll hit a bad shot. If you hit a good one, it's just plain luck.

That's one reason for taking a little practice swing first. You should set in your own mind *exactly* what you intend to do with that chip shot when you take your practice swing. Then stick to your decision when you actually get over the ball. If it turns out you made a mistake, learn from that mistake. But if you are always indecisive, your chipping, too, will be indecisive.

On your practice swing, take it nice and easy. Then try to duplicate your practice swing when you hit the ball.

In general a chip shot should just barely reach the green and then roll the rest of the way to the cup. As long as we stick to our four-club method you will have two irons to choose from: a No. 5 iron and your No. 8 iron.

The No. 5 iron, having less loft, will naturally produce a shot with more roll than a No. 8 iron. Where the pin is up close and a No. 5 iron will roll past, take your No. 8 iron.

But, where there is a choice of clubs, always take the least lofted club that will get you to the green. There's a good reason for this.

When you try to chip the ball up close to the pin, a lot of things can go wrong. Perhaps your ball doesn't have enough backspin and keeps on rolling. Greens will vary and perhaps your ball will hit a soft spot and stop, or a hard spot and keep going. When you play a rolling shot, the ball has a much better chance of overcoming irregularities on the green.

Finally, don't forget your putter. Many times when you

are just a foot or so off the green, your putter is your best "chipping" club.

Before we go on to another subject, remember these chipping tips: Make up your mind during your practice swing and stick to your decision. Be firm and decisive in your actual swing. But, above all, don't rush the shot.

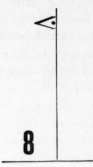

8

Escaping Sand Traps

ONE OF THE SHOTS which gives the beginner m[...] trouble is getting out of sand traps. The rules, of cour[...] won't let him ground his club, and this tends to confuse hi[...] Then, too, very few amateurs practice bunker shots, so wh[...] they get into a trap they have very little experience to gui[...] them.

Now the best way to handle the problem is to keep out [...] traps in the first place. You cannot avoid every sin[...] bunker, of course, but in a surprising number of cases you [...] find your ball in a sand trap because you took an unnec[...] sary gamble.

You tried to reach the green by pressing your shot inste[...] of playing short and safe. Or you grew careless on an a[...] proach shot and dubbed it.

Since you will always need at least one stroke to get o[...] of a trap, you should treat bunkers for what they are—g[...] hazards. If in doubt, play your shot so even if the ball does[...]

50

go precisely where you hope, at least it won't land in the trap.

But, since even the best of plans don't always work out, you should learn to master the art of escaping from sand traps.

Actually a good deal of the problem of a bunker shot is mental. The inexperienced golfer is afraid. But once you have mastered the proper technique, this can be a very valuable shot. As a matter of fact, I will often deliberately aim a shot so that it will go into a trap if I'm a little off line, rather than chance another approach to the green that might easily go out-of-bounds or lose me additional strokes.

At this stage in your game, when your ball lands in a sand trap you should be concerned about only one thing—getting out in one stroke.

If you are an over-100 shooter, the chances are that you will waste a half dozen strokes a round trying to get out of bunkers. Let's start working now to "save" those strokes.

If you are in a trap that is level with the fringe of the green and your ball is sitting on top of the sand, consider using your putter. There is no rule saying you have to explode out of a trap. As a matter of fact pros use their putter in a hazard whenever they can. We often call this club a "Texas wedge."

If you've got a good trap lie, a chip shot may be the answer. Except that you can't ground your club in sand, it is played like a chip shot off the fairway. As I reminded you in the last chapter, if you chip out of sand, take your time and don't rush the shot.

If neither putting nor a chip shot is advisable, then you must explode. This is especially true if your ball is partially buried, or if there is a lip to the trap that might catch a ball chipped out.

There is one essential difference between an explosion

shot from a bunker and every other shot in golf. Ordinarily the club head strikes the ball first and then takes a divot in its natural arc. In the bunker shot, however, the *sand is hit first*. The force of the sand against the ball "pops" it out of the trap.

Then too, while you normally have good footing on a golf course, in a sand trap your feet are less secure.

In order to be sure of hitting the sand you should aim the club slightly *behind* the ball. And because of the loose footing, take time to wriggle your feet in the sand until you get a good firm purchase with your spikes.

Also, to insure firm footing, take a wider stance than normal with the particular iron you are going to use. With your four-club method, you will choose a No. 8 iron for your sand shots. Later, of course, when you add other clubs you will want to carry a sand wedge for traps.

Now the explosion shot used by professionals is the one which I think most amateurs can learn rapidly. It requires a few extra adjustments but is a surer way to escape from a bunker than any other method.

This is a "cut" shot and it is exactly what the name implies. The club head *cuts* under the sand on which the ball is resting. Because it cuts under the ball there is far less chance of "burying" the club head into the sand and muffing the shot.

The cutting action is produced by hitting from *outside* the line of flight.

Now, so that you will understand exactly what you are trying to accomplish, let's go back to one of our early lessons when we laid an extra club down on the ground to represent the line of flight we intended the ball to travel.

When you swing a No. 4 wood, for example, the club head automatically stays on the inside of that line because of our turning movement. Then, you recall, when we came to the chip shot, we talked about taking the club head back along the line of flight so that we went directly to our target.

In the cut explosion shot the club head should come from *outside* the line of flight as it strikes the ball.

In playing an explosion shot we should "open" the club face. That's simply golfing language for increasing the loft of a given club. Here's all you have to do. Take your normal stance with a No. 8 iron. Now turn the club so that it points slightly to the right of your target.

Next, release your grip and re-form it properly with the V's pointing toward the inside of your right shoulder. (This is necessary because in turning the club your V's have got out of line.)

All right. The final step is to change your stance to a more open position. This is necessary because the club face is pointed to the right. In order to bring it around so that it is again square to your target, you must move your body so that you face more toward the hole.

A short cut is to take your stance so that you are turned 45 degrees, halfway toward your target. Then grip the club so that the blade is squarely toward the hole. I used the longer description so that you might try it step by step and understand the principles involved in the short-cut method.

Be sure, however, that you wind up with the club face square to the target. Too frequently golfers take the proper stance, facing halfway toward the target, but they let the club face point to the right—and that's the way the ball goes when they swing. Or they may easily "blade" the ball on the sole of the club and knock it a mile.

The ball should be played just about off the left heel on the outside of the line. Remember that we want to strike a *descending* blow in order to pop the ball out of the sand and onto the green.

As to how far you should strike the sand *behind* the ball,

you have a good deal of latitude. If you swing properly you can hit anywhere from an inch to a couple of inches behind the ball and still get it out of the trap.

But—since this will become important later on—I want you to get in the habit of hitting from a half-inch to an inch behind the ball. Get this stroke as grooved as the others in your game because later on we'll want to use it as the basis for the finesse bunker shot.

The most important single feature of a sand shot is that the club head must go through the sand smoothly and evenly. Too many players do everything right, except that they "quit" when the club head hits the sand.

There is only one remedy for this common ailment. You should keep your hands firmer on the grip than normally. I don't mean to keep them rigid—but be sure they are firm enough to withstand the shock of hitting the sand.

The other thing to strive for is a smooth, even tempo to your swing. Like a good chip shot, a sand shot shouldn't be rushed. Nor can you be lazy. You must be decisive.

Let's review the principles once more because this bunker shot, one of the easiest on the course for the experienced player, often gives the beginner the most concern.

We'll play this shot off our left heel.

We'll take a more open stance than usual—turning so that our body is open about a half turn.

We'll place our feet wider apart than usual and set them firmly in the sand.

We'll make sure the club face is pointing squarely at our target; adjusting our hands so the V's are pointing properly. This will "open" the club face.

We'll take about a three-quarter swing, with the backswing going slightly outside the proposed line of flight. The club head is picked up abruptly.

Then with a firm, even tempo we'll bring the club head down to strike just behind the ball.

And we will follow through.

I don't expect you to pick up this lesson as fast as the others. Only repetition will make this shot "automatic." But once you learn it, you'll come to regard it as just another problem on the golf course.

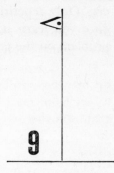

9

Putting with Confidence

ONE OF THE TRUEST statements in golf is that tournaments are won, or lost, on the putting green. When we pull out one of those sub-par rounds that win the big ones, it's generally when our putter is "hot."

For any player good putting is the fastest way to cut your score. When you can eliminate three-putt greens from your game, you are getting down into the expert class.

Of course you can't afford to neglect any phase of your golf game if you really want to become first rate. Good play from tee to green must always be your goal.

But until you've gained experience, it stands to reason you are going to make your share of errors on the golf course. You can recover from many errors on the fairway, often without loss of a stroke. But a bad putt is a stroke thrown away which you can never recover.

Unfortunately many golfers will work diligently only on

56

their driving and long shots. Of course there is a certain satisfaction in belting out a good drive.

But, to be realistic about it, you are only going to use your driver fourteen times, at best, in a round of golf. The way par is figured, you will putt thirty-six times in eighteen holes.

In other words, if you three-putt every green you will use up fifty-four strokes. That doesn't leave you much margin to get from tee to green and still break 100, your current goal. On the other hand if you cut down to two putts per green, you'll lop off eighteen strokes from your game right there.

There are many styles of putting, each of which has proved effective for some golfer. If you are a good putter, don't change your method. I don't care how unorthodox it may be; if your style of putting works, stick to it.

But if you are having trouble with your putting, try my way and see if it won't improve your scoring.

Actually every good putting method has the same basic ingredients:

1. Picking the right line and distance to the cup
2. A dependable putting stroke
3. Confidence

I cannot overestimate the importance of confidence. If you approach your putt with doubts, those doubts will be translated into your judgment and putting stroke. It then becomes pure luck if the ball drops.

When you start telling yourself, "I can make this putt," they'll begin dropping for you.

All right. How do you gain confidence? Actually this isn't as hard as you might think. Let me tell you why.

A great many people assume that the top pros sink 20- and 30-foot putts as a matter of course. Now, occasionally we do and then the sports writers make a big to-do about it in the papers.

But the payoff putts for most of us are those short ones—

six-foot and less. We don't make all of them, either, any more than you do. Still, putts of this length are the ones we *should* make, and *so should you*.

When you drop the short ones with fair consistency, your confidence will start building up, and you'll be lagging those long ones up for the short tap-in putts.

While we're talking about confidence, let me mention one other point. There are golfers, even on the tournament circuit, who will never become consistent money winners because they lack confidence in their putting.

They are always blaming their bad luck on their putters. I know one pro who carries in his car as many putters as I have golf balls. There are others who always carry two putters in their bag, which to me makes about as much sense as carrying two drivers.

Fellows like that are always experimenting with a new putter instead of facing up to the real problem, which is simply *to master one*.

Now I myself carry a second putter in my car. It is almost identical with my regular putter, except that it is slightly lighter. If I run into a particularly bad putting streak, I may switch over to the lighter one. But if I don't find any marked improvement (and I usually don't), I go back to the old one. And believe me, I wouldn't give up that reliable old putter for all the tea in China.

I prefer the mallet-type putter. I can hit a golf ball with it more easily, and that extra weight gives me better "feel" and confidence. It also seems to me that I get a truer hit, particularly on the long putts.

It is not so easy to line up putts with this club, however, and you may prefer the blade type. Try out both kinds and pick the one which seems to give you the better "feel." But then stick to that club until you master it, or until you are sure the putter is at fault, not you.

In my time I've experimented with just about every kind

of putting stroke. In the old days the pendulum stroke was well thought of. There are many fine putters who still use this method. However, it is a much longer stroke and I, for one, feel that there are too many ways in which I can go wrong with it.

Until about 1954 I used to crowd over the ball and take my grip down the shaft. Then I found there were "too many parts" to my putting stroke. When I had a tough 7- or 8-footer, my crouched position seemed to open the door to a lot of faults.

Since then I've used a long putter and stand more upright with the ball close to my feet. This position suits me best and my scores have improved as a result.

Plainly enough, my style of putting will not automatically turn you into a top-notch putter. My system won't work for every golfer.

But I will say this: It gives you a lot less room for error, and, unless you are already a fine putter, my system should be an improvement over your present method.

First of all, let's consider the grip.

Some professionals putt with the same grip they use for every other club. They stress the obvious advantages of sticking to one grip from tee to green.

However, I myself prefer the reverse overlapping grip originally known as the Bobby Jones grip. It is essentially the same as my regular grip, but instead of the right little finger overlapping the left forefinger, my left forefinger overlaps my right little finger. (Hence the name "reverse overlap.")

In the reverse overlap all fingers of the right hand grip the shaft of the putter.

I hold my left hand slightly "open." My thumbs are down the shaft; my right thumb slightly to the left of the shaft. But, most important, the backs of the two hands are square. This is vital because a good putting stroke is based on hitting the ball squarely along the proposed line of roll to the cup.

I even go a step further, and I think you should try this too. I try to remain *square* throughout the entire putting stance. My feet are from eight to nine inches apart and *square*. My toes are an equal distance from the proposed line of roll.

My hips are square. So are my shoulders.

Finally, to give myself the firmest possible foundation, I rest my forearms on my hips—my left forearm against my left hip, my right on my right hip.

As I said, I use a 38-inch putter, so that I stand up fairly straight and the ball is right at my feet. If you hunch over quite a bit (and do so, if this position feels more comfortable to you), then naturally the ball will be farther from your feet. Yet regardless of your stance, make sure your eyes are directly over the ball.

One reason I stand more upright is because I get a better perspective of my putt that way.

My style on short putts is strictly a wrist action. Everything else remains stationary.

I start with the back of my left hand square to the proposed line of roll. I take the club head back along that proposed line of roll by breaking my wrists and bring it back along that same line, again with only my wrists moving.

It is almost a hingelike movement of the wrists. On short putts I have found that the less action of the shoulders and arms, the less margin there is for error. I keep my nerves and my swing intact by relying solely on my hands.

In terms of "feel," my right hand is doing the putting. The left is the guiding hand, and the back of this hand should start and wind up square to the proposed line of roll.

Actually on the short putts, my stroke is more of a "tap."

In watching other golfers, I have reached the conclusion that on short putts most of them use entirely too much action. You'd be surprised how little backswing is needed to hit a ball four feet.

Further, it stands to reason that the less backstroke you use, the less chance there is for your club to waver or your stroke to "come apart." The tap stroke is also a firmer and stronger type of putting. The club head shouldn't come back more than, say, six inches.

Most of the money players today are using the short tap stroke. They feel that if they take the club head back only a few inches, there is very little that can go wrong, providing they have a good firm grip.

When you practice the "tap" put a tee in the ground six inches in back of your ball. Then work until you can stop your putter before it hits the tee on your backswing.

Or here's a method I've used in my room at home. I stand up near a wall or the leg of a chair and make sure I stop short of the distance I've allowed myself. This enabled me to deliberately shorten my putting backstroke.

In putting, as with every other stroke in the game, don't rush your shot. If you hurry, particularly with the tap stroke, you will slap or "stab" at the ball. Strive for a smooth, even tempo.

Also, don't "quit" when the club head strikes the ball. Let the club head follow through. Your putting stroke should be firm and decisive.

And above all, keep telling yourself, "I can make this putt."

Here's a little psychology I use on myself in practice. I never aim for the hole when I'm working on the practice green before a round. If the ball didn't happen to drop, I might lose confidence.

So, rather than putting for the practice cups, I pick out a spot on the green—a slight discoloration, a light spot, a slight mark—any type of target, and aim for that.

I spend nearly all my practice time on putts up to about

six feet. I start out with a foot, then a foot and a half, and gradually work my way back from the target. Every once in a while I'll practice a long putt, but usually I concentrate on the short ones because, as I said earlier, tournaments are won and lost on short putts.

If you want to think like a golf pro (and that is what I am trying to teach you), you ought to follow the same routine: Practice your short putts until you drill them into the back of the hole with reliable consistency.

There are two common reasons for missing short putts. The same reasons apply to pro as well as amateur golfers.

One fault is "overreading" a short putt.

The second is trying to "baby" the ball into the cup.

If you use the tap-putt method and hit the ball crisply, it is not likely to be thrown off line. As you practice (and as you putt on a regular round) hit your short ones so that even if they miss the cup, they will go past it by about six inches.

Never leave a putt short. If you do there is absolutely no chance for the ball to go into the cup. If you putt a little harder than you should, there is always the chance that the ball will drop.

Now I don't mean you should knock them a mile past the cup. But see that you err on the side of being too long, rather than too short.

The tendency to "overread" a short putt occurs when the green slants between your ball and the cup. Quite clearly, if the green isn't level, you've got to allow for some roll—either to the right or the left, depending upon the slant.

Now here's a valuable little tip for short putts that I've picked up while playing thousands of holes of golf. If you figure you should aim an inch above the cup so that the slant of the green will carry the ball into the hole, *cut that margin in half and hit it firmly.*

In other words, if your first reaction is to play the ball an inch above the cup, aim only a half inch above. Your perspective on short putts will tend to make you overallow for the break in the green.

It is wise also to form a habit of aiming toward the "high" side of the cup. In other words, if the green slants so that the right edge of the cup is higher than the left, aim for the right edge. That way you give the ball a chance to drop in, even if you are a little off line.

Usually the professional will "err" on the high side, the amateur on the down side. In fact this is what we mean by the "pro" and the "amateur" sides of the cup.

But, above all, hit those short ones firmly and decisively This minimizes the effect of the greens and, most important, gives your ball every chance to drop into the hole. I get my share, maybe more, of those "lucky ones" which drop even though they aren't hit perfectly. But I've given my ball (and my luck) every chance to work for me.

On the longer putts, I use more arm motion. I take about the same stance as I did for the short ones, except that I stand slightly pigeon-toed. I don't think there's any advantage in this, except that it makes me feel firmer in my stance.

On long putts I use a slower-paced stroke with less wrist action. Instead of a tap stroke, my long putts are more of a stroke. But I confine my movement to my arms and wrists. The rest of my body remains as stationary as on the short ones.

On a long putt you should have only one objective: to get the ball close enough to the cup so that you are sure of sinking your second putt. I occasionally drop one of those 40-footers, but that isn't my objective. I'm simply trying to lag the ball up for a sure two putts.

What I don't want to do is putt so short, or so far off line, that I have a three-putt green.

I'm not going to spend time here telling you how to "read" a green. Right now you shouldn't worry too much about picking the exact line to the cup, particularly on a long, tricky putt.

I'd rather have you concentrate on the most important problem—gaining the right feel for distance. If you learn to putt for distance, even picking slightly the wrong line won't hurt you much.

But if you leave your longer putts short, you'll wind up more than six feet from the cup and increase the odds that you'll take three putts on that green.

So instead of aiming for the hole on long putts, aim for a three-foot circle around the cup. If you've worked enough on your short tap putts, you know you can sink the ball if you get it within three feet. So make that circle your target.

Nobody can teach you how to judge distance with your putter. It is strictly a matter of feel and the only way you can acquire that feel is by practicing.

There are, however, some simple rules you can follow. If you are putting uphill, be a little more decisive. And ease up a bit if you are putting downhill.

If you are using a putter from the fringe of the green (remember I said that this was one of the better "chipping shots") be a little more decisive because the rougher fringe will "hold" the ball back more than the smoother putting surface of the greens.

And by all means follow the pointers I have given you.

On a short putt, putt firmly and with confidence.

On the longer putts, aim for the right distance so that you leave yourself no more than a three-foot second putt.

In every putt, keep your body firm. Let your hands do the work on the short putts; your hands and arms on the longer ones.

Above all work so that you *can* say to yourself on every makable putt, "I can sink this putt."

Pretty soon you'll be doing it, and then you'll be on your way to breaking par.

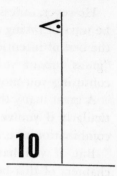

10

Straightening Out Your Golf Problems

IF I NEVER MADE a mistake on a golf course, I'd win every tournament I entered. Of course everybody makes errors. The only difference between the pro and the amateur is that the pro makes fewer mistakes and only rarely will he permit himself to make the same mistake twice in a round of golf.

Actually nobody ever makes golfing errors *deliberately*. If, for example, slicing is your problem, I know you aren't doing this intentionally. Perhaps you feel sure you are following all my suggestions to the letter. Yet for some reason or another the darn ball keeps on slicing.

If your particular golf problem persists despite all your efforts, your best bet is your golf pro. He can watch you swing and spot the cause of your trouble much more easily than you can "guess" what's wrong with your game yourself.

A great many golfing faults can be traced directly to one

of the fundamentals of golf, which you may have overlooke
A trained pro can spot such things, quickly.

However, unless you are playing with an expert, you shou
be wary of taking advice from a fellow player. He may ha
the best of intentions, but he isn't a trained observer and h
"guess" about your problem will usually only succeed
confusing you more than ever.

A great many things cause golfing errors. Sometimes, pa
ticularly if you've learned bad golf habits, you may have
combination of errors.

But, if you have worked conscientiously on the earli
chapters of this book, your problem usually can be spott
quickly. More than likely you haven't fully grasped the e
act way to employ the golfing fundamentals to your swing

Now let's take the commonest fault of all—the slic
Nearly every beginner starts out by slicing. I suspect this
because the beginner often imitates a baseball swing, wh
he first starts to play.

At any rate slicing is the most frequently encounter
problem of newcomers and 100-plus shooters. It is also
fault which has a very simple basis, and it can be quick
cured.

First, let's see what happens to the club head in the corre
golf swing. The club face is square to the target at addre
When it returns to strike the ball, the club face should aga
be square, just as it was at the start.

Secondly, the club face should strike the ball on an a
from inside the proposed line of flight, traveling toward t
outside. This produces a spin on the ball that causes it
have a slight hook.

A bad slice results when the club head neither strikes t
ball squarely nor with the slight inside-out arc. You sli
generally because your club face is open and your swing
coming outside-in as it hits the ball.

Usually this is caused by a bad grip, and that was one reason I stressed the proper grip in an earlier chapter.

Most instructors note that chronic slicers do not point the V's of both hands properly toward the inside of the right shoulder.

If you suspect that this may be your trouble, stand before a full-length mirror. Take the grip which seems natural to you; then look in the mirror. Try this several times with different clubs to find out whether you are forming the grip properly *or only think you are.*

There is also a second form of bad grip. Let me illustrate. Take one of your clubs and form your regular grip. Now turn your hands to the right so that the V's point more toward *the outside* of your right shoulder.

Note what happens to the club face when you turn your hands to the right. The club face has opened up. If you hit the ball with the club head in that position it will slice and fly off to the right of your target.

This problem usually arises because of a failure to take the club back properly at the very start of the backswing. Instead of swinging it back in a one-piece swing, the golfer has started back by picking up the club with his hands.

Here's the "T" trick I use to check my own swing.

Tee up your ball for your drive. Now put another tee in the ground about a foot and a half in back of the ball and inside the proposed line of flight.

Now swing your club head back. If you are doing this properly, your club head should strike that second tee. If you aren't striking that second tee correctly, find out why. You are either picking up the club or you are swinging too far outside the line of flight.

Experiment with that second tee in various positions until you are consistently swinging the club head back in the proper arc.

A bad hook is only a rare ailment of the beginner and

100-plus shooter, so I'll just mention it briefly in passing. One of the most common causes of a hook is having the left hand too far over to the right. Then on the downswing the wrists tend to roll and close the club face on impact.

You have probably noticed that beginners often miss the ball completely. This is almost invariably caused by looking up. If you pull up your head just as the club head is about to strike the ball, the whole arc of your swing is raised. Then you either miss the ball completely or top it.

Of course there are a host of troubles that can result from faulty balance. Hitting behind the ball is one. Hitting the ball on the neck of the club instead of the club face is another. A wild hook or slice are still others.

If you are having trouble "feeling" the proper pivot, here is an exercise that will help. Stand with your heels shoulder-width apart, and with the proper stance—left toes out, right foot square.

Now just clasp your hands together in front of you, elbows bent. Next, simply pivot to the right and return. You have no club or golf ball to concern you. All you are doing is practicing your pivot, so observe closely the shift of your weight and your foot and knee action.

I've known pros to practice this for hours, drilling into their muscles the feel of the right weight shift and turn.

This exercise is a good cure for "dropping" your left shoulder on the backswing. (I run into that problem myself on occasion.)

Dropping your left shoulder is a special hazard for golfers like me who use an upright swing. If you aren't careful your left knee "collapses" and drops that left shoulder and head. This lowers the plane of your swing, causing you to hit the ground before you hit the ball.

In addition to the faults of hooking and slicing which are obvious on a long shot, there are "miniature" versions of the same problems on your short approach shots.

A ball which flies off to the right of your objective is caused by an open club face. With a longer club this would result in a slice.

The ball that flies off to the left has been hit with a closed club face. It is really a baby hook.

Some golfers are inaccurate on their approaches because they put too much pivot into their short iron shots. Remember that these shots are played mostly with the shoulders, arms and wrists, but with little hip turn.

This is particularly true of your chip shots. The club head should be brought back and through the ball on the proposed line of flight.

If you scuff the ground on a chip shot, there are usually two causes. You've hurried the shot. Or you haven't kept your weight primarily on the left side.

Dubbing your explosion shot is also often caused by a tendency to rush your swing. Another common bunker error, quitting so that the club buries in the sand, comes from letting your wrists go slack at impact and not making a conscious effort to follow through.

You may also hit too far back of the ball, so that the club head either digs into the sand or, even if you follow through, your swing lacks the force to overcome the resistance of the sand.

Only experience can cure this problem. The difficulty stems from the fact that you can't ground your club in a sand trap. This tends to make you unsure, so you rush your shot. Let your waggle help to smooth out and slow down your tempo.

Dubbing a shot out of thick rough comes from bad judgment and bad execution. If you are in trouble, always remember to take a club with enough loft to get you out. Too many people will choose a No. 5 iron when a No. 8 is the "safe" club.

Then, having picked the wrong club, they dub their shots

by trying to "kill the ball." Instead they should let the loft of the club do the work for them.

Getting the loft of the club to work for you is good advice everywhere on the course. The player who tries to "stretch" his clubs by overswinging or speeding up his tempo, usually throws his entire game out of kilter. And, instead of getting those extra yards he hoped for, he winds up hitting short of where he would have gone with normal effort.

Putting errors usually come from stabbing at the ball or from a loose grip that requires you to regrip the putter at impact. Be sure you have a firm but not tense grip and take a firm, decisive stroke at the ball.

And even the "tap" putt requires the club head to travel through the ball. You can't just bring the putter to the ball and quit.

Also be sure you have a firm foundation for your putting with feet, hips, and shoulders square. On the short ones let your wrists do the work. But, above all, don't tense up. You can't stroke a golf ball properly if your muscles are locked tight.

Here's a brief review and check list for the trouble spots to investigate in your swing:

1. Your grip
2. Your left heel and right elbow
3. Are you swinging the club head back rather than picking it up?
4. Is your grip firm at the top of your backswing?
5. Are you bringing the club head down with your hips and shoulders and releasing your hands last as they go through the hitting area?
6. Are you keeping your eye on the ball, but letting your head move up with the natural pull of the follow through?

One final point. So far in this book I have not emphasized keeping your left arm straight because this advice has been exaggerated by too many instructors.

Of course, you should keep your left arm *reasonably* straight. The straighter the better, as a matter of fact, because the left arm and hand guide the swing.

But you shouldn't try to keep it so straight that your muscles become too tense.

On the other hand don't fall into the other trap of allowing your left arm to "hinge" at the elbow. Instead, just let your natural pivot bring the club head back to the top of your swing.

And now a last word. When you run into any golfing problems, remember what the pros do. The first thing they check is their grip. Most times that's exactly where the fault lies.

11

Playing Tips for Breaking 100

THERE ARE TWO essentials for the player trying to break 100 consistently. One is mastery of his clubs. The second is learning how to think properly on a golf course.

If you have practiced diligently with the No. 4 wood, the No. 5 and No. 8 irons, and your putter, you are making progress toward mastery of your clubs. As I have stressed, this doesn't happen overnight.

Once you have reached a degree of proficiency with these four clubs, then add your other woods and irons. But always use these basic four clubs as "landmarks" for judging distance and performance with the rest.

I have tried, as we've gone along, also to start you on the second important path: thinking like a champion. As your game gets better and better, correct thinking on the golf course will become increasingly important.

Now I'm not going to minimize the mental block that occurs when you try to break 100 consistently. This is one of golf's biggest hurdles. It is particularly difficult because at this stage you probably still lack confidence in your game and this shows up in missed shots.

I'm no stranger to pressure, either. Every big tournament brings pressure, especially when thousands of dollars are riding on a single shot. Yet the pressure I feel is no greater than that of the golfer going for that shot or putt which will finally bring him below 100.

Now one of the things I do is try to know my own game. I try to find out exactly what I can and what I can't do on a given day. There are days when I feel relaxed and everything goes right. There are others in which my confidence isn't up to snuff.

If I come to a tough spot, I rely on the club that has been working best for me that day.

Now let's see how this kind of thinking applies to your game.

First of all, you know you are going to make a certain number of mistakes during a round. As a matter of fact, if your course par is 72, you can make up to twenty-eight mistakes in a round and still break 100.

But—and this is the important thing—you want to make as few mistakes as possible.

That leads us to lesson No. 1: Take no unnecessary gambles.

Let me illustrate. On the first hole you've hit a fair drive and a pretty good second shot. Now you have 150 yards left to the green.

If you hit a perfect No. 5 iron, you'd land on the green. Then two putts and you'd be down in five. And, say, that's par! Boy, oh boy, if you can pick up a par right off the bat, you'll have some extra strokes to spare later on if you need them.

But wait a minute.

Let's take another look at that 150-yard shot. Can you

consistently hit a No. 5 iron 150 yards? Or do you need a little luck riding with you?

Now let's take still another look. What will happen if you don't quite hit that No. 5 iron as well as you think? Where will it go?

A slice—if that is still giving you occasional trouble—will mean hitting into those trees. That's tough enough. But also, you'll have to play over a trap coming back. If you go in there, it will take at least another stroke to get out.

Now let's add up that score. Three strokes into the trees; one out and into the trap; one out of the trap. Now two putts and you have a seven and with any bad luck, probably an eight.

On the other hand, what happens if your No. 5 iron is just a little short? The ball goes into a sand trap. If you explode out perfectly, you've lost nothing. But are you sure of exploding out of sand traps perfectly every time?

No, the chances are you'll get the ball out, but still leave yourself a chip and two putts to get down. So once again your score adds up to seven.

Now, suppose you don't take that gamble and, instead, deliberately play your shot just short of the traps, or, better still, near the opening between the traps that guard the green. Now you've left yourself either a short approach or chip shot. Two putts and you are down in six.

By eliminating the gamble you have saved at least one stroke, maybe two or three.

All right. Let's take a look at the next hole. We'll assume that it is a dog-leg to the left. There are thick trees and rough on the left. If you hit a good drive you'll be past the bend with a clear shot for the green.

But what if you don't hit that good drive? If you're short, you'll still need another shot to get past the bend. If you hook, the ball will go into those trees for either an unplay-

able lie or a bad enough spot so that it will take you one or
two strokes to get out.

If, however, you play off to the right, the green "opens up"
for you automatically. True, it is a long second shot away
but you can get home easily with your No. 4 wood even if
you don't hit it as well as you sometimes do.

Now on the third hole your drive goes into the rough. If
you hit a good No. 5 iron shot, you'd be in perfect position.
But how many times do you hit a good No. 5 iron from the
rough? On the other hand, you know you can get a No. 8
iron out of there with no trouble at all.

I have not taken isolated cases. Players who shoot over
100 are "giving away" anywhere from 10 to 20 shots a round.
Actually you'd have to be a 79 shooter on all your other shots
to give away 20 strokes in a round and still break 100. You'd
have to be an 89 shooter to give away 10 strokes and still
break 100.

That just doesn't make sense, does it?

All right. Here's the formula (and it is one I use myself
in money tournaments): What do I gain if I make a given
shot? Then, what will I lose if that shot doesn't come off the
way I plan?

Let me illustrate with hole No. 16 at Tam O'Shanter. It
is one of the toughest holes in the country and has often
been called the "graveyard" because so many pros have seen
their chances of winning the Tam Open or World go aglim-
mering right there.

It is a par 3, maybe 220 yards long. You shoot over water
to a long but narrow green. The pin is on the right side
and is guarded by a huge bunker. A creek runs along the
left and in back of the green.

The water hazard in front is no problem. I know my
shot will carry that without any difficulty. The bunker, of
course, *is* a problem. But—and this is where I made my

decision—the biggest danger is to the left. If my ball goes too far left it will land in the creek.

I couldn't afford to waste a stroke with a shot into the water. So I decided to aim for the green, taking a chance on carrying that bunker.

This exact situation came up in the final round of the 1957 World. It so happened that my tee shot was just about a foot short of the green, and the ball rolled back into that bunker.

From there I exploded out and sank a five-foot putt to give me my par.

Had I gambled and gone in the water, I never could have made my par, and the wasted strokes would have cost me the title and $50,000.

Just as I can't waste strokes and win tournaments, so you can't throw them away and keep on lowering your score.

Now, as you improve your game, you can take more chances—only they won't be chances any more. When you know for sure that you can hit a consistent No. 5 iron, there is no longer any reason to have doubts. You will have taken the gamble out of that shot.

Now I have no intention of turning you into a patty-ball golfer who is content just to shove the ball along hole after hole. Nor am I expecting you always to play super-cautious golf. It wouldn't be much fun to start with and, besides, it wouldn't lay the groundwork for your next goal, which is to get your game consistently down below 90.

What I am saying, however, is that you should eliminate all the gambles where the odds are against you. The gambles in which you risk two or three strokes in hopes of maybe picking up one.

That isn't good percentage golf.

Now the second place to cut down on your scores is on the putting green. Here again golfers throw away strokes unnecessarily. Particularly on your long approach putts, make sure you get them up to the area around the cup.

If in doubt, putt a little stronger on those long ones than seems right to you. Most amateurs putt short, and as we've already seen, a short putt gives you no chance for that lucky drop.

Be bold too with your chip shots. Play them firmly and decisively. If you can put that chip up close to the pin for a lay-in putt, you've saved a stroke.

Learn to play your own game from tee to green. If you are in a foursome with a long-ball hitter, don't worry about his game. He's got his own problems too. Your goal is simply to play the best game *you* can.

The pros have an expression, "Playing within yourself." By this they mean playing your own game, the best game of which you are capable. This is especially wise advice for the high-handicap player.

Then, too, learn to play one shot at a time. If you dub a shot, forget it. That's one mistake you made. Try to avoid making it a second time. But don't compound one mistake with several.

Now I'd like to stress one other point about thinking good golf. Every time you hit a ball you ought to be learning something. You ought to be studying the course so that you know it intimately.

In a single practice round a pro doesn't pick up the points about a given course by accident. He's looking for landmarks to judge distance. He's filing away information about the location of traps; he's finding out where trouble lies on the course.

He's also photographing in his memory the details of the various greens. He's trying to pick out the "easy" way to play the course when the tournament starts in earnest.

Unfortunately a great many golfers will play their home course year in and year out and keep making the same mistakes in strategy. They never seem to learn that there is a built-in pathway from tee to green.

They regard the golf ball (or their golfing companions) as the opponent, rather than the course itself and the goal they've set—whether it be 100, 90, 80, or par.

To summarize what I have said in this chapter:

1. Don't take any unnecessary gambles.

2. Play your own game.

3. If you make mistakes, forget them. Try to avoid making the same mistake twice in a round.

4. Spend time to *know* your home course.

5. Keep the ball in play.

One final reminder: Don't forget to warm up before you start out. A little time on the practice tee will save you strokes when the scoring counts. The same is true of using the putting green for a rehearsal of the putts which come later on the course.

The place to leave your errors is on the practice tee and green.

PART II

PART II

12

Analyzing the 90 Shooter

THERE ARE TWO KINDS of golfers who shoot in the 90's. There is the man we've been working with in Part One of this book—the beginner or the plus-100 shooter who has got his game down under 100.

That golfer will usually continue to improve because he now has a pretty sound evaluation of his game. He knows his strengths and his weaknesses. In order to lick the 100-barrier, he has worked at fundamentals and at his mental attitude toward the game.

In this second section of the book I'll show him some more pointers to keep that score shrinking.

But there is another kind of 90 golfer as well. Chances are he skipped through the opening chapters of this book because he didn't think they concerned him.

However, the average 90 golfer is what I call a "sometimes" golfer. He is sometimes in the 90's, sometimes in the 80's, and—on a bad day—he's over 100 by a stroke or two.

That means his game will vary possibly fifteen strokes between a good and a bad day. Such a variation means that his game is better than average, but it isn't consistent. He has the makings of a good golfer, but hasn't yet developed a reliable game on which he can count.

Many golfers are satisfied to shoot in the 90's. This is a respectable score at any country club. If you can play golf only occasionally and haven't the time or inclination to work at your game, you have no appologies to make in any company for a game in the 90's.

But the 90 shooter is a man who can be helped, probably more easily than any other golfer. He usually has a good concept of the game; theoretically, at least, he knows the details of a good swing. Usually he has golf "savvy" because he has played enough to have gained experience.

In fact he has the makings of a par shooter, which is the goal all serious golfers are aiming for.

There is no such thing as *the* 90 shooter. Golfers who shoot in the 90's have a good deal of variation in their faults —the reasons why their game has stabilized, at least temporarily, in the 90's.

But in my years of playing with high-handicap amateurs I would say that the typical 90 shooter plays something like this:

He is likely to hit for satisfactory distance on his drive, but usually has a slice or a bad hook. Most of the time his fault doesn't give him too much trouble because he's learned to live with that slice or hook and take it into account when he aims.

But he loses several strokes a round when a slice or hook doesn't come off the way he expected.

He will waste a stroke or two on a bad fairway shot, but most of the time a shot that wandered off the fairway really cost him strokes and distance.

On good days his putts are dropping and his short game

is consistent. But there are days when this part of h
isn't so hot and his score goes up.

Finally, he usually has one (sometimes two) bad hol
which cost him double-bogeys or worse.

And then there are days in which nothing seems to go right
and his whole game goes sour. The only thing that keeps him
coming back another time is a good drive or a fine approach
that restores, temporarily, his hopes that tomorrow will be
the day when everything goes right and he breaks par.

Unfortunately that day never comes to the golfer who
waits and hopes for a miracle. Golf is a demanding game
and luck can only help you a little.

The 90 golfer who wants to get his game down into the
80's, and then into the par-breaking range, has to clear away
the cobwebs of fundamental faults and wishful thinking on
the golf course.

In many ways he is like the player we discussed earlier in
this book who was either just taking up the game or who had
struggled in the over-100 category for a time.

The 90 golfer who wants to improve must eliminate the
basic errors from his game, eliminate the loss of unnecessary
strokes, and sharpen up his golfing thinking.

As I mentioned a moment ago, the 90 golfer has a great
asset—he has experience and his game is still mobile enough
so that he isn't too set in his golfing ways to change.

So now let's get busy and change that "sometimes" in the
80's to a game in which you are "consistently" in the 80's,
the next step toward shooting par golf.

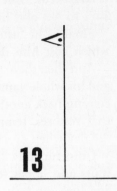

13

Improving Your Swing

WHENEVER I VISIT a country club, there are always three questions which I am asked:

"How can I improve my swing?"

"How can I reduce my score?"

"How do you get as much speed as you do with your club head?"

Yet, when I ask other professionals the commonest fault of their 90 shooters, I invariably receive these answers:

"They have a poor grip, but it's hard to get them to change because they are so used to it."

"They have very bad footwork."

There you have the dilemma of golf. The professional has the answers to the questions which members raise. The solution is waiting for them in the pro shop and on the practice tee. But, instead, many amateurs keep looking for a new "miracle" answer to better golf.

In Part One of this book we devoted considerable attention to the problem of the correct grip. I urge you to reread that chapter from time to time because a correct grip is an indispensable ingredient of a correct golf swing.

Let's assume that you are reasonably sure your grip is correct. The V's of both hands point toward the inside of your right shoulder, the shaft is gripped in the palm of the left hand, the fingers of the right.

However, the place for the 90 shooter to check his grip is at the top of the backswing.

The beginner and the over-100 shooter check their grip and stance at address. This gives them a reasonable guarantee that if they swing the club head properly during the first four or five feet of the backswing, the rest of their swing will be all right.

This is sound theory, and this is still the best check point for the 90 golfer who finds himself occasionally posting a score over 100.

We have tournament pros who look like Joe Duffer on his once-a-month trip to the municipal links. You wonder how in the world they even hit a golf ball, let alone hit it well enough to earn a living on the circuit.

The answer is simple. They have learned their own game so thoroughly that, although they make what most of us consider mistakes, they compensate for these mistakes in their swing. You probably have at your home course such a player —the fellow everybody chuckles about when they first see him, but not after he posts his score.

That man actually has remarkable golfing powers, because he is canceling out his errors as he goes along. Somewhere in his downswing, he corrects all the errors he made going back. And that's quite a trick.

Unfortunately, most golfers who have an offbeat style last only as long as their coordination and strength correct their obvious mistakes. The record books are filled with golfers who hit the top for a brief moment, then faded away when

they could no longer compensate for the basic errors in th
swing.

So the advice I gave beginners and 100-plus shooters
Part One is equally good for you who shoot in the 90's. T
ing the club head back in a compact, one-piece swing is
sential for every good golfer.

But the way you take the club head back becomes un
portant unless at the top you are ready for the pay-off pur
—the swing at the ball. I could take any top-notch pro a
position his club at the top of his backswing and he wo
hit a good, consistent drive—even though he hadn't had
thing to do with bringing the club head back.

In other words, I expect you to take the club head ba
properly. I assume you already do this. Now, what conce
me is the position in which you have placed yourself af
you have completed your backswing. Your left arm sho
be reasonably straight. Your left wrist should be cocked a
bent so that creases appear where the hand and wrist join.

The left hand should be grasping the club shaft firm
particularly in the little finger. The right hand should
under the shaft. The right elbow should be pointed do
toward the right hip pocket.

Your weight should be on the inside of your right leg w
somewhat more weight on the right than on the left si
I'd estimate that my weight at this point is about 60 per c
on my right side, 40 per cent on my left.

The hips should have made their turn; the should
turned so that the left shoulder is under your chin. Y
head should be directly over the ball, chin cocked sligh
to the right.

The right foot should be firmly planted with the wei
still, as much as possible, on the inside spikes. The left f
should have rolled over onto the instep, with the heel on
near the ground.

The club-head position at the top of the backswing is

portant. If the club face is pointing to the sky it is "closed." If the club face is at right angles so the toe of the club is pointing to the ground, the club face is "open."

A square club face at the top of the backswing will be about halfway between open and closed. In general the toe of the club face will be pointing toward the ball.

If you swing the club head back in a one-piece movement and arrive at the proper point at the top of the backswing with a square club face, your objective now is to return your hands as near as possible to their original starting position at address.

One other action can also take place. You can "pronate" your wrists. The low-handicap golfer should know this trick. But for now it comes under the category of a golfing error.

"Pronating" simply means "turning" your wrists. Some golfers, instead of taking the club head back with the back of the left hand square, will roll the wrists over so that as they pass waist high, the wrists turn to the right. Now, on the downswing the wrists must turn back to the left again to return to the original starting position.

This is quite a trick, even in the hands of an expert. It is often the reason why high-handicap golfers slice some shots and hook others without any definite pattern. The ball either hooks or slices depending on whether your wrists turn back to the left too little or too much.

The "cure" is to make sure you take the club head back squarely and firmly with the cocking of the wrists coming after you have reached the completion of your hip turn.

Now that we've set the top of the backswing as the place for the 90 shooter to check his swing, let's see what errors in position he can make and what happens when he does.

The weak grip in the left hand is a very common error. We've discussed how this error (recognizable by a loose left little finger) results in "throwing the club" from the top. This in turn either causes the hands to uncock at the very beginning of the backswing, or creates a looped swing. The first results in a weakly hit ball, the second in a slice or hook.

The second error is a "flying" right elbow. Instead of pointing down, it points out to the rear.

The "collapsing" left arm results from completing your backswing, not by turning your shoulders, but by bending your left arm at the elbow. This shortens the arc of your swing, and causes you to lose distance. It also makes the arc of your swing indefinite and may cause your shot to go every which way.

How your weight is distributed at the top of your backswing is also important.

Here are the commonest errors of balance:

1. Weight too far forward.

Cause: starting out with the weight on the balls of the feet instead of back on your heels, or stiff (instead of slightly bent) knees. This makes you fall "into" the ball on the downswing. The resulting shot is either hit on the neck of the club, poorly hit, or dubbed.

2. Weight too far to the left.

The 90 golfer starts out with his weight primarily on his left foot and *keeps it there* during his backswing. This results in the golfer leaning toward the target on the backswing, then leaning *away* from the target on the downswing. This as you have already seen, is a common reason for hitting the ground in back of the ball or of topping your shot.

This is a common fault, so some teaching pros insist that their students make a definite shift of their weight to the right.

I don't follow that school of teaching because I believe it leads too easily into the fault of shifting weight by moving the entire body laterally to the right.

Your weight should move to the right side on the backswing, but only because your hips and shoulders have *turned* to the right. They haven't *moved* to the right.

The basis of every good golf shot is proper balance. Your weight should be on the insteps of both feet; your knees should be bent and your body in perfect balance. Note in this picture that the V's formed by my grip are pointing toward the chin. An instant after this picture, I use a slight forward press to get my swing started.

The follow-through is the check point most instructors use to judge a golf student's game. If the golfer retains good balance, if the essentials of a proper swing have been executed, then the final stages of the golf swing follow naturally. A "picture" finish means that you've properly executed the earlier phases of your swing.

A firm, steady footing is essential to conquering the problem of escaping from sand traps. Note that my feet are firmly set, my knees slightly bent. You will also notice that my stance is open so that I am facing more toward my target.

This photo shows a rear view of the same stance for a sand wedge shot. Observe that I have gripped down on the club slightly. This is one of golf's handiest shots, once you have mastered it.

The sand shot is the mark of the expert, and it can be learned easily.
Confidence and a few golf fundamentals are involved. The essentials are good balance, control of the club throughout the swing, and
patience to take it easy. Don't rush this shot, but do it crisply and
with assuredness.

The secret of escaping from sand traps is a firm, sure stroke. The test is your follow-through. In the picture you will see that I still have complete control of the club even though the club head has already traveled well through the sand and the ball is on its way toward the cup.

Many times a chip shot from a sand trap is your best bet. In a fairway trap, you can often use a longer iron to avoid losing distance to the green. Note, however, that the same principles are involved: good footing, balance, open stance, and full control over the club throughout the swing.

The putting green separates champions from "also-rans." I credit my putting skill to the essentials illustrated here: square stance, square hips, square shoulders, and forearms resting on my hips for a firm foundation to my putting stroke.

Here is my stance for the longer "approach" putt. I still rely on a square stance, but I use more arm movement for this stroke than for the short ones. Square stance, shoulders, and hips are vital to a confident stroke to send the ball on true line to the cup.

This lateral shift may result in some pretty long drives if the weight has shifted properly. The fault—and it shows up in the amateur and, eventually, in the guilty pro—is that you've got to shift back precisely as much on the downswing. That kind of shifting can get pretty tricky, and if your reflexes aren't precise, you wind up with a hook or slice. You may also get a ball that flies abnormally high in the air with no distance, or a topped shot.

There are a lot of ways to visualize the correct swing. I liken it to turning a doughnut around on your forefinger. Your forefinger represents an imaginary line from the top of your head down through your body into the ground. The doughnut is the action of your hips and shoulders.

Your hips and shoulders are revolving around an axis—in this case the imaginary line from top of your head to the ground.

If you are turning, instead of swaying, you'll feel your weight in both your insteps throughout the backswing and most of the downswing.

Now let's go on to another point. I don't want to get too technical about the golf swing, but some basic understanding of the swing is essential not only to help you spot your faults but also to reassure you when you are swinging properly.

The club head, in the backswing, goes from a position on the ground to a point where the shaft is roughly parallel to the ground. In effect it has traveled about three-fourths the way around an imaginary circle.

As you swing the club, it will retrace that same distance and travel on around until it winds up at the very end of the follow-through. From the beginning of the backswing it will have completed one entire circle and more than half of another.

If you took sequence camera shots of your swing so that the club head appeared in regular timed pictures, it would show this: The club head moves back smoothly on the backswing, neither dragging nor rushed. On the downswing the club-head speed gradually accelerates.

It reaches its maximum speed in the last few feet before it strikes the ball. This is because the earlier movements came from hip and shoulder action; the hand action was delayed until the last segment of the swing.

The club head travels through the spot where the ball was and gradually loses momentum in the final stages of the follow-through.

Now if you took these pictures and put them all together on one page, the club head would form an arc—the path it covered from address, through the backswing, down through the swing and follow-through.

This pattern is the "arc" of your swing. If you add the shaft of the club to the picture, it forms a "plane" as you remember from your high-school geometry.

If you took a side view of this arc or plane, viewing it from behind golfers looking toward the target, you would find it varying, depending upon the player.

The more the arc or plane approaches a straight up-and-down line through the ball, the more upright the swing. The more it drops down toward the ground, the "flatter" the swing.

Now I myself have a fairly upright swing. As a matter of fact, I'm always trying to "flatten" it out a little for more power and to offset a tendency to drop my left shoulder.

A heavy-set golfer generally will use a very flat swing.

There is more power in the flatter swing, but it also creates the problem of "round-housing." The more upright swing can produce greater accuracy for the golfer whose build will adjust to it.

The proper arc is something which you have to work out for yourself to fit your height, weight, and general build. If you follow the earlier instructions for stance, backswing, and checking the top of your backswing, you should settle automatically into the right plane for your particular swing.

There are, however, two further checks you can make to see whether your judgment is correct. If you continue to slice even though your grip and backswing position appear sound, you may be using too upright a swing.

On the other hand if you are "reaching" for the ball at your address and feel off-balance during your swing, you may be trying for too flat a swing. This usually results in a hook, but can sometimes (in extreme cases) give you a slice.

Now, while I have stressed the position of the club, hands, and body at the top of the backswing, I do not want you to "pose" at the top of your backswing.

As I mentioned in the chapter addressed to the beginning golfer, I can't stop my swing at the exact moment when I've reached the top of my backswing—and nobody else can, either. That's why the notion of a "pause" between the backswing and downswing is inaccurate and dangerous advice.

I can stop just before I reach the top of my backswing, or just after I've started my downswing. The little "extra" is the coiled feeling I have in my body, particularly in my leg and stomach muscles.

I feel "coiled," just like a spring that is tightly wound, and when I unwind, I'll have the power of first my body and then my hands to propel the golf ball toward my target.

This "coiled-up" feeling is one reason why I cautioned against a slow, deliberate backswing, and also against going back too fast. It should be a steady, smooth-flowing swing, much as you might draw back the bow in archery or draw back the leather pocket in a slingshot.

In my case the backswing is, as I've said before, about two-thirds as fast as my downswing. In any event you should go back at a speed which gives you rhythm, perfect balance, and at the top of your backswing a feeling of coiled power in your body.

Remember the sequence: on the backswing the hips, arms, and hands move together; the hips complete their work; then the hands cock.

On the downswing the sequence is the same. The hips move, bringing the arms down along with the hands (still cocked); then the arms, and last the hands uncock through the hitting area.

On the downswing I feel that I'm getting my left side "out of the way" and that I'm holding back my hands until the very last instant.

In Part One I suggested that beginners and plus-100 shooters get themselves a weighted practice club. I encourage every golfer to follow that advice. Work with this heavy-weight club until you get the "feeling" of the right swing.

Then apply that instinct to your regular clubs and watch your score melt away.

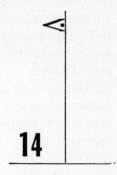

14

Judging Distance

THERE ARE TWO common methods of judging distance
—one in yards; second, the distance you get with a given club.

I myself seldom think of how many yards I have left to
the green. By experience I know instinctively what club
will automatically carry me the required distance. Sometimes, particularly when you are playing a strange course
for the first time, yardage becomes about your only guide-
post.

But even here you should start learning distance in terms
of your clubs. If, for example, on a strange course you find
a par 3 with the distance rated at 135 yards, try to compare
it with a similar 135-yard hole on your home course. What
club do you use there? If the hole varies from your home
course because the green is elevated, or lower, add or sub-
tract one club.

I'm trying to stress this most important lesson in thinking
as a professional does: Learn to see distance in terms of what

yardage you will get with a given club and a given swing.

If four pros all congregated on a certain spot of a golf course, all of us might "guess" at the exact yardage and be fairly accurate. But you can be sure that each one of us would accurately decide the proper club we need to carry that distance.

Now we might not all agree on the same club. From 90 yards out, we might use a No. 8 iron, No. 9 iron or a wedge, depending on the individual characteristics of our game. But each one of us would know the right club for him.

Without watching you play, I couldn't tell you exactly what club to use from a given distance. You yourself must learn that through experience.

Of course a golfer can have no accurate judgment of distance if one time he hits a No. 5 iron 150 yards, the next time 140 and, occasionally gets only 135 yards with that club. His "yardstick" is too stretchable.

That is one reason why I emphasized in Part One the four-club approach—to learn and master four clubs: the No. 4 wood, No. 5 iron, No. 8 iron and putter.

With the three distance clubs you have a yardstick to work from. Even the 90 shooter, I think, can benefit by concentrating on these same four clubs because they are a foundation for every other club in your bag.

To judge distance effectively, you must create some kind of foundation—a given club and given swing that produces a certain distance. Then you judge every other problem from that known quantity.

There are, of course, aids.

Some golfers will check the distance on their score card and then pace off the distance of their drive. After doing a little arithmetic they know almost exactly the distance remaining to the green.

Some courses also have yard markers.

Another trick is to pick out an object a certain distance

away; decide how far it is, then multiply that distance by what you observe when you look at your target.

Other pros will select a prominent object like a tree alongside the green and judge its distance from their ball. And here's a further tip: On well-kept private courses the distance across the fairway from rough to rough is 45 yards.

Most pros, of course, judge distance from experience. However, if I lay off for a while I've got to readjust and as I play, my sight and judgment of distance sharpen up.

But I've found only one really sure way to judge distance.

In Part One, you remember, I explained the routine I follow on every shot.

I judge my problem as I walk up to the ball, while I am taking my practice swing (from behind the ball and in the direction of my target) and as I address the ball.

But, if there is any question in my mind about the shot (and there often is), I do one additional thing.

I walk up behind my ball and survey the situation which confronts me. At this point I may make a tentative selection of the club to carry me "home." If I'm positive, I will then take my practice swing and complete my routine.

However, if there is the slightest doubt, I walk up ahead of the ball to a distance which I recognize as a spot from which I know the shot needed. On a short approach, for example, I'll walk up to a place from which I *know* a No. 8 iron is the correct club to carry me to the green.

Then I glance back at my ball to check the distance I have walked ahead and add enough club to carry the extra yardage I need.

In other words, I take a known factor (how far I will hit a ball with a given club), go to that spot, and then figure how much more club I need to carry the remaining distance.

Finally, as I walk back to my ball, I'm reviewing my decision. I make one final check as I take my practice swing. (One value of the practice swing is to give you time to re-evaluate your judgment). Finally, when I assume my stance for my shot, I am certain in my opinion, and any doubts have been erased.

In my business, professional golf, we are constantly moving from course to course. We have to learn distance-judgment fast in a practice round or two. If you play one course regularly you will have a big advantage—provided that you take full use of it. You will be able to check and recheck time and time again what we pros have to learn in a big hurry: judgment of distance in terms of what each shot in your bag produces on a given hole.

On a practice round I note where my tee shots land on every hole. I then pick out some object—a tree, a bush, a bunker, a light spot on the fairway—any landmark.

Then, when I play a tournament round I'll remember whether I was 15 yards short, or 15 yards past that landmark on my practice round. I'll remember whether I hit the ball well or not. And I'll remember whether the wind was in back of me, into me, or across.

For a pro, the object of a practice round is to find out where he is hitting the ball. He may never hit that particular spot again in the four rounds of a tournament, but at least he's got a landmark to go by.

If I played a No. 4 iron from a given spot one day, and the next time my tee shot was 10 or 15 yards nearer the green, I know I've got a 5-iron shot left.

Later in the book I'll give you some pointers on playing a completely strange course which you have no time to study in advance.

But if, on your home course, you gradually learn to pick out landmarks and build up judgment about how and why the ball landed where it did, you will be gaining the ability to judge distance in terms of your own game.

Start now. Every time you hit a ball on your home course, learn all the other pointers I have given you about stance, swing, and the mechanics of golf. But also learn to "think"; add to your store of knowledge of how not only to play golf but how to play your particular course.

Golfers can play hundreds of rounds and improve the mechanics of their game. But a smart golfer will learn with *every* round, and learn to *think* while he learns to *play*.

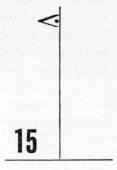

15

How to Get Your Best Drives

A GREAT MANY golfing instructors will attempt to minimize the drive. I've pointed out that the driver is one of the clubs you will use less frequently than your putter and, as a matter of fact, it may get much less use than your No. 5 iron.

This is very true, of course.

But, frankly, I know of nothing that gives you a better start on a confident round of golf than a good drive on the first tee. You and I both know that one shot doesn't make a round; but it sure is a big help to my morale to get started right.

The trouble with a great many golfers is that they simply don't have time to practice. If you are busy all week long making a living, you only have weekends to play; and you aren't going to waste that time practicing.

I know this. That's the reason I've stressed taking a little time each day in your backyard to work on grip, stance, and swing. If you have time to work on the practice tee or driving range, fine. A serious golfer will somehow find that time.

But, since I've attempted to make this book as practical as possible, I know that some golfers will jump into their car, rush to the golf course and, after a few practice swings, tee off.

Now most times, they could start out a half hour ahead of time and leave an interval for the practice tee and green. *And they should.* Those few extra minutes are very important.

But things don't always work out that way—even for a pro.

During the 1957 Open I thought I was to begin playing at ten o'clock. I drove leisurely to the clubhouse and strolled in. Suddenly somebody said, "You're supposed to tee off."

I thought they were kidding.

Then I looked out at the tee, and sure enough there were the rest of my threesome waiting.

I raced into the clubhouse, tossed on my shoes (I didn't even have time to tie the laces), and ran out to the tee. I took a hurried practice swing and drove off.

Luckily I hit the ball fairly well. It landed about twenty yards short of where I would normally have driven. I composed myself as I walked up to the ball and I hit a fine second shot, a No. 3 iron, about fifteen feet in back of the pin.

I putted out without any trouble and when I teed off at the second hole I was ready to play. I was lucky that my lack of preparedness on the first hole hadn't cost me any strokes.

I say it was luck because that is rarely the way it works out. Too often a golfer will rush to the first tee and take a few practice swings. He isn't ready to start a round of golf yet but he does anyway.

He usually winds up frittering away shots on the early holes. If he's lucky, he'll settle down before too much damage is done. But after a poor start, he may just keep on play-ing poorly all day long.

From my experience, I would say this: If you have only a limited time each week to play golf, you ought to be more—not less—careful of how you spend it. If you've got all week to work on your game, it doesn't make as much difference if you throw away one whole round of golf.

It is, of course, never wise to play poorly whether you have all the golfing time in the world or not. But it seems to me bad judgment to take the once—or maybe twice—a week that you can get to the golf course and then, for lack of a few minutes' preparation, play a poor round and rob yourself of the enjoyment of a good game.

So, whenever possible, allow yourself a little extra time to get ready before teeing off.

But, as I said before, this isn't always possible. Perhaps the alarm clock doesn't go off; or, on a Saturday morning, it isn't always so easy to crawl out of bed in time for your match, let alone a few minutes earlier for practice. So whether you practice in advance or not, get as ready as you can for that first shot—the one which may set your golfing mood for the whole day.

That first drive on the first hole is where most golfers suffer the greatest case of the jitters.

Let me tell you about a time when my jitters were particularly bad even though in this case my troubles did not come on the first tee.

We were playing the 1954 National Open at Baltusrol. At the end of three rounds I had 212 and Ed Furgol had 211. I was playing well on the final 18 holes when I got to the last tee.

If I made a par I'd wind up with a 284. Assuming I made a birdie (although I hadn't on that hole in any of the previous three rounds) I'd wind up with a 283—a figure which looked good enough to win.

When I teed up, Ed Furgol (the man I had to beat) was playing the 8th hole. I felt that if I put a 283 on the board, the pressure would be on Ed and the others still out on the course, and they'd have a tough time catching me.

The 18th is a par-5 hole and a dog-leg. I decided to go for a par, figuring that a 284 would win; if I got lucky and made a birdie I'd post what ought to be an untouchable total. I'll cover this point more fully elsewhere in the book, but for now let's agree that psychology plays a big role in winning —and losing—tournaments.

If you get in early with a good score, the pressure is on the players who are still out on the course. They are then forced to gamble, and when you gamble things can often go wrong.

Up through 17 I was coasting along in fine fashion. I was playing good golf without pressure. I had hit an iron on 17 that I thought might be in trouble, but it cleared the bunker. I hit a good chip shot from the fringe to within a foot or a foot and a half of the cup and sank my putt.

But suddenly on 18 I felt the pressure building up. Now I knew that I had this tournament in my hip pocket. Naturally I got a little tense. Sometimes this tenseness is controllable; sometimes it isn't.

At the same time the people on the course heard that I had a 284 going and might win the tournament. So there was a sudden influx of spectators coming from all over. We didn't have sufficient marshals to control them.

A half dozen photographers also made an appearance.

Up to that time I had been driving especially well. I had no reason to "doubt" my driver at this stage of the tournament. But—

On 18 the whole left side of the fairway is guarded by tremendous trees that grow right down to the ground. The fairway is straight, but hilly.

To the right is rough and extremely to the right are fir trees.

While my playing partner, Bob Toski, and I were getting ready, the gallery started to move in. They edged out into the teeing area. I tried to tee my ball up on the right side as the officials struggled to move the crowd back. But they couldn't move because they were packed in too deep. As I looked out down the fairway, all I could see were heads.

So I started to worry. My nerves aren't too good at this point, I thought. At least they aren't good enough to start hitting a full driver over the heads of my gallery.

So I moved to the left side of the tee.

When I did this I "blocked" out all the trouble. There is also a creek which runs parallel to the fairway on the left side. The creek is the one thing you've got to avoid.

There's an old saying in golf that if you tee off on the side of trouble, you'll shoot away from it. This I did by teeing on the left side; however, from this spot I partially blocked from view some of the fairway. But, most important, I had eliminated the problem of shooting over the gallery.

Well, somewhere in the swing something went wrong. As I look back on it, I think I probably tried to check my swing at impact because of uncertainty. There was also a lot of confusion on the tee, and one version is that a spectator yelled just as I started my downswing.

The details aren't important. If I had had full control of my nerves and concentration, somebody could have set off a cannon, and I'd have never heard it.

As a matter of fact, I should have waited another five minutes for the officials to restore order at the tee. But I didn't want to test my nerves that long. I was afraid I might lose my concentration. So, rather than let my nerves get any more jittery, I went ahead and played my shot.

I picked a bad place to tee off from. Actually it wouldn't have been too hard to reach that green in two. But from where I teed off I left myself a tough drive. I had to hook the ball slightly to get the ball into the fairway.

Whatever the cause and effect, I wound up by hitting a very poor tee shot; I sliced into the trees.

Then I drove a provisional ball that it turned out I had to use. For my first tee shot wound up in an unplayable position at the foot of a tree.

I needed a seeing-eye dog to find the ball in the first place, and when I did I would have needed an ax to play it out. To cut a painful story short, I wound up with a seven.

If I had simply made my par I would have tied Furgol. A birdie would have won the open for me.

I've dredged up this golfing nightmare simply to show you that I've suffered from the jitters, too; and I appreciate the problem which confronts many golfers.

The first tee shot is a particular problem for the beginner. He believes that every person around the tee is gathered there for just one purpose—to jeer when his drive is dubbed. These are jitters of the worst kind.

The experienced golfer knows that few onlookers are watching. They are more concerned with their own problems; usually they are thinking about the tee shot which they'll be making themselves a few minutes later.

On the other hand the 90 shooter will take this occasion to suddenly review in his mind nearly everything he's ever heard about golf. This is the one shot he isn't going to miss. (That one on the 18th at Baltusrol was the one *I* wasn't going to miss, either.)

So he thinks about weight shift, grip, left heel, right elbow; all the many components of a good golf swing. He makes only one mistake—he doesn't think about the most important thing of all, which is simply to hit the ball.

Now you never completely relax on that first shot. I'm just as excited today as when I first hit a golf ball in a major tournament. When I stop getting excited, I'm sure I'll be "through" as a money golfer because the tension is part of the game. I mean I care enough to play well.

Properly channeled, this "tension" is helpful. It helps m
concentrate on the job I'm doing—hitting the first shot in
round of golf. It also gives me a competitive edge that
invaluable in tournament play.

I believe that the practice swing is one of the finest ways t
channel this tension into productive golf. If I'm at all ner
ous, I try to settle myself down during that practice swin
If I'm going to make any errors, that's the time to do i
when I'm not hitting a golf ball.

One of my tricks of concentration in times of jittery ter
sion is to try to clear my mind of everything except hittin
the ball. I use the preparation time for selecting my clu
choosing the angle of my shot, and all the other details.

Then I devote all my thinking processes simply to hittin
the ball *exactly as I did in my practice swing;* because ove
the years I've found that my practice swing (since it doesn
count) is usually pretty reliable.

If you've taken time to warm up on the practice tee, th
chances are that you've grooved your swing well enough s
that your stroke will be pretty well set by the time you sta
your match.

But if you've had to rush to the tee, here's a suggestio
Take a few warm-ups with your No. 8 iron. It is light an
short enough to limber up some muscles. Now move to th
No. 5 iron—which is a little longer and little more deman
ing. Next, move to "old reliable," your No. 4 wood.

Finally, swing your driver a few times to get completel
loosened up.

Now it is your turn to tee off.

Put your ball on the tee; and forget it for a moment.
necessary, take a deep breath to relax your muscles (an
your nerves). Now, ignoring the ball, step back about
yard behind it and take a practice swing—remembering t
aim in the direction toward the flag which you should fo
low with your regular swing.

Don't rush through this practice swing; don't make it just "routine." Concentrate as if you were actually going to hit the golf ball. One practice swing; two at the outside, are enough. Too many and you will defeat the purpose.

Now walk up to the ball, just as you've done dozens and dozens of times on the golf course. Look at your objective (the flag) as you take your address. Waggle. Then swing the club back and hit the ball.

Don't try to "baby" it down the fairway, but don't try to belt it a mile, either. Try to divorce all thoughts except that of hitting the ball squarely and decisively.

Sometimes it won't go right. Shots don't go right for me all the time, either. But the more you learn to concentrate on that first shot, the more frequently you'll be off with a good shot.

Above all, never rush it. Some golfers feel subconsciously that they've got to tee off right away for fear they are holding up the people waiting at the first tee.

Quite clearly if you get off a good tee shot you'll be out of the way a lot faster than if you dub one and have to take a second swing at the ball a short distance from the tee.

If you *must* concentrate on anything on that first tee shot, let it be your natural swing back from the ball. Remember the lesson I gave beginners about the importance of that first few feet of your backswing.

But don't concentrate so hard on this that you follow the club head back with your head and sway away from the shot.

By the time you get to the second tee you've had a few golf shots under your belt and your muscles are loosened up. Even so, the same rules apply.

Tee your ball up and forget it. Use your practice swing to limber up, to "think," and to get ready. Then let your actual tee shot follow without worry or doubt.

Let your confidence extend to your clubs. The manufac-turer who produced your driver put a lot of time, money, and research into producing a club which would perform its function of getting the ball into the air and down the fairway.

Your role is simply to swing that club properly.

A driver, as we all know, has the least loft of any wood in our bag. So it will produce the lowest-flying ball and the greatest distance.

Sometimes our drives go haywire—not just one tee shot, but several. In this case, particularly if you are producing a low-flying ball with little distance, it may be wise to switch to a No. 2 or No. 3 wood for driving until your confidence is restored.

If this fault persists, however, you should consult your pro because your driver may not be suited to your game, and you need a replacement.

There are also times, particularly when the wind is behind you, that you will want to use a more lofted wood for your tee shot in order to get the ball higher into the air. I want to stress, however, that the driver is usually the club you should employ, and if you find yourself working with other woods, it is time to re-evaluate your game.

A drive, because of the distance the ball travels and because you employ a full swing, is probably the best single "laboratory" test of your golf swing. If you have a golf error, it will show up more clearly and more decisively on your drive than on any other shot in the bag.

If, therefore, you find errors in your driving, refer back to the chapter on correcting your mistakes; because the flaws in your driving are more than likely also present elsewhere in your game, but less easily recognizable.

But don't "tinker" unnecessarily with your game because of only a few bad drives. I don't always hit the "perfect" drive, and nobody else does either. We just do the best we can and we only take our game apart when our driving is *consistently* off.

I want to touch on one more point about driving before we go on to another subject. Probably nowhere in golf is there such a temptation to "keep up with the Joneses." If you are a man with average reflexes it is "insulting" to have another golfer in your foursome consistently outdrive you.

A woman in a mixed foursome is also conscious of this feeling. She knows she can't drive with most men, but the temptation is there nonetheless.

I don't attempt too often to match those 300-yard hitters. *I play my own game.*

I do this from tee to green. If somebody else outdrives me by 30 or 40 yards, more power to him. A big drive looks fine, but they pay off on the scoreboard for the number of strokes taken from tee *through the green*.

Learn your own capabilities and stick to them. That's good golf advice anywhere on the course, but especially on the tee where the temptation to "belt one" is so strong. If you are a long ball hitter, fine. If you are not, don't worry about it, and, above all, don't try to "stretch" your own capacity. It can only lead to trouble.

Driving alone has never won a major tournament for me yet, and it probably never will if distance is the only gauge you use. But *accurate* shooting from tee to green has won a lot of matches—and it will pay off for you too.

16

Mastering Your Fairway Woods and Irons

On a par-5 hole and the long par 4's, you generally need a long second shot to get close to the green. Depending upon the distance involved and the lie of the ball, you have a choice of a No. 2 wood, No. 3 wood, No. 4 wood, No. 5 wood, No. 2 iron, No. 3 iron, or No. 4 iron.

In our basic four-club approach, we used a No. 4 wood for the long second shot. I still rely often on this club as my fairway wood, and particularly when the ball is in the light rough.

With a perfect fairway lie, most professionals will use a driver for their second shot. However, this club should be used only by the low-handicap player; the inexperienced golfer will have difficulty getting the ball into the air with it.

Few pros even carry a No. 2 wood. If the fourteen-club

limit is raised, we might go back to it. But, even so, I don't think most amateurs should bother with a brassie.

A No. 3 wood will give you almost as much distance and it is a much "surer" club to use. As a rough rule of thumb, you can figure about 10 yards difference between each club in the bag.

A No. 5 wood is an excellent club for most players to use in the rough. Now, obviously I don't mean in the heavy going, because when you get into the tall stuff your only choice is a club with plenty of loft to get you out back on the fairway.

But in light rough the No. 5 wood is very handy. You should use it in preference to an iron. Unless you have very strong wrists the blade of an iron is likely to "block" on the shot or skitter off line when it encounters the resistance of the grass. The No. 5 wood, on the other hand, has a heavy knobby head that sweeps through with enough momentum to hold its line.

A No. 2 iron, as we have already seen, is one of the most difficult clubs for most players to master. It is useful when you learn to handle it properly, but this takes time. Meanwhile you are usually well advised to select a wood whenever you feel you have an option.

With my woods I take the same slightly closed stance that I use with my driver. My heels are about shoulder-width apart.

I use a square stance with the No. 2, 3, and 4 irons, narrowing the distance between my feet slightly with each succeeding club.

With the fairway woods and the long irons, take a full swing as you do with your driver. You recall that I play the ball from the same position with each shot—about two inches to the right of my left heel.

Just as in driving, the principles of the swing and weight

shift are important and they are handled in exactly the same way. It is also essential to take your time.

Many golfers are in too big a hurry to hit the ball. They are always conscious of players behind them on the course and try to speed up. Nobody, of course, wants to play any slower than is necessary.

But if you'll establish a routine for every shot, you'll find that it doesn't take much more than a minute, and you'll hit a surer shot for having planned it carefully.

With a long second shot that won't reach the green, my routine is fairly simple. As I walk up to the ball, I analyze the situation. I walk up ahead of my ball just far enough to get a good look at the pin. I want to know if it is set on the right side of the green, the left, or in the middle.

I look at the green—where does it open up; where is the trouble; what will be the easiest and best spot from which to play my third shot?

If I determine that I want to be on the left, I pick out some object—usually a tree or bush—in back of the green and use that as my target.

And all the time I've been walking I have been thinking about my choice of club. I walk back and pick out my club, take my practice swing behind the ball in the direction I intend to play my shot; then I step up and swing.

At no point do I hurry; nor do I take any undue time. It is simply a matter of habit. I follow essentially the same routine on every shot and I've done this so often it becomes automatic.

With the long woods, the ball is literally swept off the ground with the club head. With irons, however, there is a definite hitting-down-and-through-the-ball action.

Frequently beginners fall into the error of trying to pick the ball up cleanly with their irons. As a result they don't strike the ball squarely on the club face and the resulting shot lacks backspin. *Let* the loft of the club produce the proper height to your shot.

You should take turf with every iron shot, even when you tee up the ball for a par-3 hole. The divot is a good check on your swing. It should start at the *front edge* of the ball.

Occasionally I run into trouble with my irons by hitting in too deeply. What happens is that I throw too much weight over on my left side by ducking my head a bit.

My shoulder has pointed too much toward the ground. As a result I hit the ground before my club head hits the ball. This loses distance or squirts the ball off on an angle. When a pro hits one that doesn't go the required distance, he says he hit the ball "too fat."

When I get into this trouble, my divot is about a half inch deeper than it should be. When that starts to happen, I recheck my swing and try to flatten it out a little so my shoulders turn more parallel to the ground.

I don't think you should *try* to take turf on your iron shots. Rather I think you should use the divot as a check point on your iron game to see that you are swinging correctly at the ball.

With the fairway woods and the long irons, it is important to remember (as you do with your drive) to take the club head away smoothly in one piece. Because you stand proportionately closer to the ball, there is a tendency to pick up your club with your hands on the backswing.

This is just as fatal a fault as it is when you drive. Here again you can use a tee, placing it in the ground behind your ball to check whether you are swinging the club head back in a low arc.

Remember to stay with the shot. Keep the club head moving through the ball for a long, graceful follow through. Just as you did with your driver, check your swing occasionally in a full-length mirror to make sure you are in good balance and your club face is square at the top of your back-swing.

The swing with the fairway woods and long irons is exactly the same one you use with your driver. So, if you are encountering faults on your second shots, analyze and correct them just as you would a poor drive.

Finally, you should begin now to work on positioning those second shots. Many 90 shooters don't improve because they simply bang away at the ball and wait until they get near the green to start thinking about accuracy.

I'm not talking about pinpoint accuracy, because the fairway woods are distance clubs. But you should be able to place the ball on the side of the fairway you prefer in order to simplify your third shot.

The ability to do this won't come to you overnight. But if you start "thinking" accuracy now with those long shots, you will develop this skill and make it easier to keep whittling away at your score.

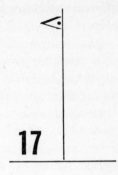

17

Approaching: the Key to Better Golf

A PAR GOLFER must have a well-rounded game from tee to cup, and that is our eventual goal. To reach that goal you must learn to master every club in your bag.

The critical stage for any golfer, however, comes in the short game—the shots from 140 or 150 yards out, down through chipping and putting.

This is the area where accuracy pays off, and errors send your scores up into double-bogeys and worse. It is also the point in your game where confidence is essential.

At the full limit of the approach shot—usually 140 or 150 yards from the green—you generally will use a No. 5 or No. 6 iron.

Beginning with the No. 6 iron, I open my stance slightly so that my left foot is somewhat farther back than my right from the proposed line of flight.

As with all shots, I'll have my right foot square, my left toes pointing somewhat toward the target.

When you reach the more lofted irons, the ball has gradually moved closer toward you because you are using clubs with shorter shafts.

Also, as your distance to the green becomes less, so does your need for power. As a consequence you gradually cut down the length of your backswing. With the shorter irons you should use a three-quarter swing, or, for the very short ones, a half swing.

After a long layoff, I usually find I'll start using too long a backswing, particularly with the short irons. There is no reason for me to take a No. 7, No. 8 or No. 9 iron back above shoulder height, but occasionally I'll bring it up almost parallel as I do with a driver. But, when I get my game back, I'll shorten my swing on every club in the bag.

The longer backswing gives you much greater margin for error. You may "turn" on your shots and let a body pivot rob you of accuracy. Then, too, your irons may lack the necessary crispness.

Selecting your club and deciding on the type of swing you are going to take is the key to a good approach shot.

As I walk up the fairway, I usually talk to my caddy or one of the other players until I'm about two-thirds the way to my ball. Then I start to concentrate as I walk the rest of the distance. I review what I know about this particular hole. What club did I use yesterday; the day before? What happened? How were the wind conditions and other factors yesterday; how are they today?

I throw my driver back into the bag, if I haven't already. Then I walk up in front of the ball to take a look. Sometimes I'll go 10 yards; sometimes 20 or 30. I walk up as far as necessary to get a good look at the green.

Primarily I am checking the location of the pin. But I'm also trying to visualize what will happen if I select a given club.

From previous rounds I know the contours of the green. Usually there is a spot on it easiest to putt from. I try to find that spot; then decide what type of shot I'll have to play to hit it.

All the time I'm getting an idea of distance because the more I look at the problem, the sharper my judgment becomes. Once I've made my decision, I walk back and take a look at the problem from behind.

I stand at my bag and start going through my club selection. I may take out one club, put it back and pick up another. I may even make a last-minute switch when I address the ball.

The important thing is that I never swing until I am exactly sure what I intend to do.

I review my decision during my practice swing.

However, if somebody else in your foursome shoots first, you've got additional time. Use it to concentrate on your own problems, not his.

In making your decision, you must first know your own capabilities. It does little good to decide where the ball should go, if you can't perform the shot properly—or if you've got to stretch your luck to pull it off.

Figure carefully your margin of error.

If you make a mistake with the club you've picked out, where could the ball go? How much trouble will you be in if the shot doesn't come off as you plan?

When you consider these possibilities, sometimes you will discover that a different club is called for to minimize the risks you are taking.

At this point you also have to start developing golf imagination—the ability to visualize the flight your ball will take in the air and what sort of roll it will have after it lands.

If, for example, you are shooting for a narrow green, will the club you have picked out hold after it lands? Or would you be better off playing a safer shot short of the green?

Naturally the more straight-faced the club you select, the more roll the ball will have after it lands.

Conversely, the more lofted the club, the less roll.

Tied in with club selection is the basic question: What iron will carry the required distance? To an extent, picking the right club comes from experience.

But—as I have stressed before—experience can be gained rapidly once you get into the habit of *thinking* and learning while you play. It is possible to play for years and never get any smarter. It is equally possible for the observant golfer to gain experience very quickly by making certain that every shot in every round of golf he plays teaches him something.

Most pros, when they get within 90 to 100 yards of the green, will use a pitching wedge. In the hands of an expert the wedge is invaluable. There is no question that today's sub-par rounds are traceable directly to this club.

Unfortunately it is difficult for the inexperienced player. Therefore, I would not advise you to add this club to your bag until you have developed proficiency with the other short irons.

But once mastered, the pitching wedge gives you the ability to hit a high floating ball to the green with a maximum of backspin. It is the tool of a golfing marksman.

In using the wedge, most professionals will employ a "cut" shot. I described this technique in chapter 8.

The essentials are these:

1. The club face is opened slightly so that it has more than normal loft.

2. You take a more open stance than you use for a No. 8 iron—about halfway between an absolutely square stance and one in which you faced your target directly.

3. The club head is brought back on the proposed line of flight, so that when it returns it will cut slightly across the intended line.

4. When you start your swing always make sure that your wedge is square to the line of flight so that you will strike the ball right for the target.

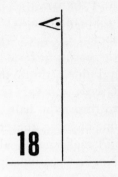

18

Tips on Chipping

IN CHAPTER 7 we discussed chip shots for the beginner and for the 100-plus shooter.

I pointed out that these short 10- to 15-yard shots from the near edge of the green can be played in a number of ways. My own style is to keep my wrists fairly firm, my body as firm as possible, and use a short backswing.

The chip shot is also called the pitch-and-run, which is a very accurate description of what you are attempting to do. A good chip shot is pitched to the green and then runs (rolls) the rest of the way to the cup.

Some players will use a pitch-and-run shot for quite a distance out instead of approaching in the orthodox manner. They aim the ball for just short of the green, counting on the resistance of the grass on the fringe to slow up their ball.

There are occasions when this is a good shot. But I rarely employ such tactics. I feel that there is too much room for error; a bad bounce or a slight miscalculation can get you into trouble.

There are also some players who prefer a wedge for their short chip shots. They aim for near the flag and count on the backspin from the wedge to stop the ball.

I don't think the percentages favor that kind of shot. Greens will vary—one spot is hard, another soft. If you try to throw the ball up to the pin and stop it, you might hit one of those uneven spots, and the ball won't react properly.

I make nearly all my chip shots with a No. 6 iron or a No. 7. Occasionally, but not very often, I will use a No. 4 or No. 5 iron. I want to get overspin on my chip shots so that if the ball hits a small indentation—a cleat mark, a spot where a ball has landed, an imperfection in the green—it will roll enough to keep going on a true line to the cup.

To do this I "hood" the club face. As you recall when we talked about the "cut" shot for the wedge, we "opened" up the club face to give it more loft. For a chip shot, we do the opposite—we take away loft.

I do this in two ways. For one thing I play the ball back more toward my right foot. Secondly, I always keep my hands ahead of the club head throughout the swing.

I take the club head back in normal fashion, but on the downswing I make sure my hands are always *leading* the club head. One way to do this is to somewhat exaggerate your follow-through. Get the feeling that you are letting your hands follow the club head low, and *stay* low longer than usual on the follow through.

The feel of this shot is entirely in your hands. You'll have to practice it a lot, but once you've mastered the trick you'll get a surer rolling ball on the green.

The effect is really to turn a No. 7 iron into a No. 6 by taking away some of its loft. This in turn imparts overspin to the shot.

Your choice of club depends on the exact nature of the

chip shot confronting you. If the pin is located close to the front edge of the green, you will naturally want a minimum roll. On the other hand, if it is set well back, you'll want a maximum roll.

The general rule for chip shots is to use the least lofted club that will get you to the green. A chip shot should land just past the fringe and onto the green. Of course, if you are already lying on the fringe, you'll have to pitch the ball part way to the cup.

Don't forget, when you are right on the edge of the green, the putter is often the best percentage club of all.

As with approaching, learn your own chipping game so that you know exactly how much roll you can expect from each of your chipping clubs. Aim for a steady, smooth tempo to your stroke.

Grip down on the club and keep your backswing as confined as possible to narrow your margin of error. Grip firmly but not tensely.

Learn a *reliable* tempo. Obviously if you hit one No. 5 iron chip hard and another soft, you will greatly vary the distance the ball will travel.

Once you have a dependable tempo, you can let your club selection do the work of carrying the ball the right distance to the cup.

19

Overcoming Bad Lies

IN OUR DISCUSSION so far we have talked generally
the good lie. Yet quite clearly, in any round of golf, you
not going to be standing perfectly level on every shot.

Here are four situations that you are almost certain
come across somewhere in your round.

1. The ball is lower than your feet.
2. The ball is higher than your feet.
3. You are standing on an incline so that your right f
is lower than your left.
4. You have a downhill lie so that your left foot is lov
than your right.

In each case the position of the ball may interfere with t
normal arc of the swing, or your weight will be imprope
distributed.

So the answer to bad lies is to compensate for these diffic
ties. There are a few minor adjustments to be made—tha
all.

When the ball lies on a spot lower than your feet, grip the club at the very end. This, in effect, lengthens the club.

I also try to keep my weight back more on my heels, because there is a tendency to fall forward when you swing from such a stance. Then too I stand a little closer to the ball than normally.

Some golfers have a tendency to slice in this situation because the position of the ball results in a more upright swing. With a very bad lie of this kind, you should allow for a slice when you aim your shot.

When the ball is slightly higher than my feet, I play it about as normally. The swing has a tendency to flatten out a trifle.

From such a lie some golfers will find it helpful to shorten their swing a bit to avoid "round-housing." This position can result in a hook that, in extreme cases, you'll have to allow for.

With a downhill lie, your weight is naturally going to be on your left side. I usually play the ball a little farther forward to offset this. Also, because it is going to be tougher to get the ball into the air, I will use a more lofted club than I normally would for the same distance.

With an uphill lie I'll move the ball back slightly more to the right and I will use a less lofted club.

There is another kind of bad lie which you run into occasionally as well. You hit a ball into the rough, and it lands close to a bush or the branch of a tree. You can't take your natural backswing without the club head striking something.

Here be sure to pick the easiest way out. Don't try any superman stunts; just get the ball out in the fairway and back into play.

I choose the club that should accomplish this, and grip down on the shaft. Then I take just as many practice backswings as I need until I can physically stop the backswing short of the branch or shrub.

If you hit anything, on your backswing, it is almost impossible to strike the ball properly. So first conquer the problem of how far you can swing; then hit the ball decisively.

Up to now we have not discussed playing from very heavy rough. Here your best bet is either your pitching wedge, or, more likely, your sand wedge. Again, use the "cut" shot to get maximum height. Make sure your grip is slightly firmer than usual as your hands and wrists are put through a very severe test. Also in this instance the arc of the swing is more abrupt.

Occasionally you will hit a ball so it lands where you don't have room to take your regular right-hand swing. This happened to me during the 1957 Ryder Cup matches in Sheffield, England.

On the first hole of the second round I pulled my second shot up against a wire fence. The only thing I could do was to take my No. 7 iron, turning it around with the toe down, and hit it left-handed with the face of the club upside down.

I got the ball out, but it went into a bunker, and I lost the hole as a result.

Sometimes a left-handed shot can be played with the back of a blade putter. But in a situation of this kind don't take needless chances and throw good strokes after bad in a hopeless case. Take your penalty and hope to make it up later on.

But above all, don't try to do the impossible. If the only safe shot is simply to get the ball out on the fairway, settle for that. Don't gamble on the impossible.

Sometimes you'll have to produce a very low-flying ball because a tree branch lies in the path of a normal shot. In this case, use a "punch" shot, similar to the one I showed you for chipping. Play the ball more off your right foot, "hood" the club face and keep your hands ahead of the ball.

Contrarywise for an abnormally high shot—for example, clearing a tree that is blocking your way—the cut shot is the answer.

There is one other kind of unusual lie. That is when your ball lands in a trap on the fairway with a considerable distance left to the green.

If you have a good lie in the trap and there isn't any lip to bother you, you can sometimes afford to take a chance with a gripped-down No. 4 wood or one of your longer irons. On this shot, the answer is intelligent club selection, a shorter, firmer backswing, and make sure your feet are well set before you swing.

20

Advanced Putting

In an earlier chapter I discussed the fundamenta[l]
of my putting stroke. Let me now briefly review the ke[y]
points in that chapter.

I use a reverse overlapping grip, which means all four fi[n]
gers and thumb of my right hand are on the shaft; m[y]
thumbs are pointing down the shaft.

I stand perfectly square; feet, shoulders, and hips parall[el]
to the proposed line of roll. I rest my forearms on my hi[ps]
and on short putts employ a short tap stroke which is co[n]
fined to cocking and uncocking my wrists.

On the longer approach putts, I use some arm motion an[d]
a little less wrist action.

A great deal of putting is "in the mind." Yet you must, [of]
course, develop a smooth, reliable putting stroke so that th[e]
ball will go where you have decided it should. Setting you[r]
self in a steady, firm position and stroking the ball con[f]

124

dently is the answer. Practice both these things on the practice greens, and on the rug at home.

The commonest faults in the putting stroke, I find, are "floppy" wrists, an "uncomfortable" stance, and uncertainty and impatience.

Your putting stroke, particularly on the tap-in putts, must be crisp and decisive. This requires firm hand action. You can't wave at the ball, lunge, or jab at it. The club head must move back along the proposed line of roll and return squarely to the ball.

Putting is a highly individualistic phase of golf, and any style of putting which works for you is all right. Too many golfers, however, are poor putters partly because they get themselves into uncomfortable positions.

Now your body plays no part in the putting stroke. If, however, you stand so that there is tension, for example, in your knees because you are crouched unnaturally, your body is entering your putting mentally at least. Your whole thinking should be concentrated solely on the putting stroke.

Uncertainty and impatience, the other two causes of bad putting, are almost exclusively mental problems. They reflect a basic unsureness of your putting stroke. The uncertain putter will usually wind up way short or, suddenly changing his mind in the middle of his stroke, will bang it way past the cup.

The impatient golfer will usually hurry his putting stroke and wind up off line.

Actually there are only three fundamentals involved in putting:

1. Picking the right line to the cup
2. Judging the distance correctly
3. Translating distance into club-head "feel"

So start improving your putting by analyzing what you are doing now. In which of these fundamentals are you making your errors?

Let's first consider your tap putts of six feet and under. If you are "rimming" the cup fairly often, there is more than likely an error in your perspective. You *think* you have the ball lined up properly, but actually you are making some small error in judgment.

There are three places this error can occur. First is when you pick your line of roll from behind the ball. Second is when you stand over the ball for your putt. The third can come from a failure to take the club head back squarely on the proposed line of roll.

You do get a different perspective of your putt while standing over it than when you line it up from behind the ball. Sometimes unconsciously you will alter your judgment slightly just before you putt and throw your stroke off line.

Here are a few tests for checking your putting judgment and stroke on the practice green. Put a small chalk mark on the green and place your ball on it.

Now stand behind the putt and pick out the line of roll you think is correct. Using another club as a marker, lay it down about a foot back of the ball (so it won't interfere with your stroke) with the shaft aiming in the direction you have selected.

Next, take your position over the ball. Then pick out a spot on or around the cup where you now think you should aim. You can usually find a little mark of some kind—a light spot or some distinctive coloration on which to focus.

Walk up and mark that spot with a chalk mark. Now, return to your ball and *again line up your putt while taking your address.* If you are satisfied that chalk mark is the right aiming point, go ahead and putt.

Let's stop and analyze these check points.

Using the two chalk marks—the one where the ball rested at the start and the point for which you are aiming—lay a club along that line.

Now compare the two lines—the one you selected from behind the ball and the one you selected while standing over the ball. Do they form a straight line? If not, your judgment has not been consistent.

Next, let's look where the ball went after you putted it. Which line did it follow—the one you selected from behind the ball, or the one you picked as you stood over the ball?

Make this test a number of times and see if your errors in judgment don't form a pattern.

Still another test is to putt a half dozen balls at a target on the practice green. If you are putting consistently, but somewhat off line, the balls will cluster in a given spot.

Picking the wrong line usually comes from a faulty judgment as you look at the ball. But it may come from an incorrect stance. You *think* your feet are square to the proposed line of roll, but actually you are slightly open or slightly closed, causing the ball to roll either a bit to the right or left of your target.

To check this, open or close your stance very slightly and again putt a half dozen balls. A very slight adjustment may be just what you need to make those putts drop.

A third error occurs when you *think* you are taking the club head back squarely along the proposed line of roll, but actually are not. Here again you can apply the "tee" test by placing a tee a short way back of your ball to see that the club head is striking it squarely on its way back.

Not every missed tap-in putt will follow the same pattern. You may sometimes miss on the left, as well as on the right. But most golfers will find that these misses aren't evenly divided—usually the greater number will "cluster" on one side or the other.

It then becomes a matter of finding out why and making the adjustment (usually a small one) to solve the problem.

Don't forget that earlier tip I gave you for short putts where the green "breaks." My advice is to make your judgment of the amount of break needed, and then cut it in half. Experience shows that most golfers "overread" short putts.

An attempt to "baby" a putt into the cup, a failure to swing the putter through the ball, and a jerky motion instead of a smooth stroke are all reasons for the putt to fall short or roll way past the cup.

We've already discussed how to combat this trouble. Taking too long a backswing for the short tap-in putt is usually responsible.

But there is another factor which many golfers tend to overlook. Greens vary considerably from day to day; even over the period of a single day. Not all eighteen greens are consistent. Learning judgment to cover these varying factors is largely a matter of experience. But a bit later on in this chapter we will give you some tips about weather conditions.

These variations will not usually have a pronounced effect on the short tap-in putts because, if you hit them decisively, the roll will overcome most problems involved in the short distance the ball has to go.

One factor which does affect putts is the grain—the way the grass is growing. When you putt *into* the grain, the grass gives greater resistance than when you are putting *with* the grain.

The easiest way to spot the grain is to study the green closely. The green looks "darker" against the grain and "lighter" with the grain. Sometimes it isn't easy to spot this from behind the ball. That's the reason you frequently see a pro walk up ahead and look back at his ball from alongside the cup.

If in doubt, a pro will also check the grain by looking at it from either side.

When you putt against the grain you should putt just a trifle more firmly to overcome the resistance. When you are putting with the grain going across your line of flight, you should make allowances accordingly.

On short putts these differences are very slight. On the longer approach putts they can become a factor. But even here they are a relatively minor detail, and you should avoid "overreading" the grain. Actually you make only slight allowances for grain. But it is one of the factors which you need to consider as you improve your putting marksmanship.

A much more important factor, particularly on approach putts, is the general condition of the greens. If they are freshly trimmed, they will be "faster."

Early in the morning, greens will be slower because the dew hasn't yet evaporated. After a shower they will be slow; after a heavy rain they will probably be very slow. In midsummer after a heat wave, even well-cared-for greens will harden up and become "fast."

While practice greens don't always reflect the exact conditions on the course itself, they will give you a good hint as to how fast or slow the real greens are going to be. So it is always a good idea to spend a little time there before a match adjusting your judgment and game to the conditions of the greens that day.

On longer approach putts, even the pro will not make a conscious effort to sink the ball. In the chapter about putting for the beginner and 100-plus shooter, I recommend that you try to place the ball within a three-foot radius of the cup so that you consistently have no more than a short tap-in putt left.

As you gradually improve your long putting, you should try to cut down that radius. In my case I putt for a one- or two-foot radius—close enough that any one of a number of factors can result in the ball occasionally dropping in.

Don't try to make the big jump from a three-foot circle to a one-foot circle. Rather set yourself first a three-foot circle, then two-foot and gradually work your accuracy down to a fine point.

The errors which exist in the short tap-in putt are also

found in the longer approach putt. The difference is that they show up more in the longer putts because the ball is traveling a greater distance.

Apply the same checks to your long putts that I suggested for the tap-ins. Check your judgment of line. Be sure that you are keeping the club face square. Because of the necessarily longer backswing, errors in letting the club face get off line can creep into your approach-putting.

Making your decision on the proposed line of roll for a long putt is one of the tougher problems of golf, especially when you get to those tricky greens with few if any level spots.

The first decision you should make in your approach putt is distance. Give yourself a target to shoot for. If, for example, you are trying for an 8- or 10-foot putt, try to get the ball within a six-inch circle.

From 15 feet, a one-foot circle, and so on back until you utilize the full three-foot radius on the extremely long putts. As you improve, you can narrow the target.

Follow our general rule of trying to err on the side of being too long rather than too short.

One advantage of putting long is that you can observe the course the ball took, making it easier on the return putt because you now visualize what roll, if any, there is around the hole. If you leave the ball short you still aren't sure what roll the ball will take.

On the relatively short approach putts there are five possibilities which you will encounter: a level putt, a downhill putt, uphill putt, a green breaking right to left and a green breaking left to right.

The level putt becomes a matter of picking the straight line to the cup and then stroking the ball for the proper distance. The others require some adjustments.

On a downhill putt you should stroke the ball a little easier than you do a level putt. How much easier, of course, depends on how much the green slants downward. Many times you have to resist the temptation to "baby" it in and leave it short.

Some pros "loosen" their grip slightly on downhill putts. Others will cut their backswing a trifle and tighten their grip.

One method that I use is to hit the ball more out toward the end of the blade. The club face isn't as lively there and so I can hit the ball just as hard as usual and it will actually roll less rapidly. This trick helps me avoid looking up through nervousness.

With a sidehill lie, you have to decide how much you should "borrow" on the slope so that your ball will curve into the cup. I try to visualize the path the ball will take. Then I pick out a spot on the green over which the ball will roll if it takes that path, and I use that spot as an aiming point.

Generally it is a good rule to take a little more "borrow" than you visualize. By going slightly above the line you picked, you leave yourself the chance that the ball coming into the hole with gravity will still fall in.

But, if you aim too exactly, your perspective changes as you get over the ball and you're apt to hit below the hole, where the ball has no chance of dropping.

In picking your line you should also have a clear picture of the action of the ball. When it starts out it has spin and momentum. It loses both in the final stages of its roll and, at that point, gravity has a greater effect on its path.

So, in judging your line, concentrate primarily on the final few feet of the ball's path where the slope will have its greatest effect.

Where I have a long 40-footer over several undulations of the green, I try to visualize the ball running. I try to figure out what the ball is going to do as it rolls over the path. Again, I take into consideration the fact that the undulations will have the least effect in the early stages of the roll; a maximum effect toward the end as the ball nears the cup.

Just as with every other shot, I have a set routine for the putting green. I walk up behind the ball, observing the general contours of the green.

Next, rules permitting, I mark and clean my ball.

Then I kneel or squat behind it to study the green, checking grain and slope.

Quite often, particularly on short putts, I walk ahead to the cup and look at my putt from the other side. This is a good check on what you've seen from behind the ball.

On the 12- and 15-footers, I also study the putt from both sides so that I'm looking across the proposed line of roll. These are makable putts for me, so I want to examine them very carefully. Quite often you can't see all the undulations of the green from either behind the ball or looking back at it. Sometimes you'll spot little rolls you hadn't noticed before by studying your putt from the sides.

Also, it is often easier to spot the grain from the side than it is from behind, or ahead of, the ball.

I make my decision before I step up to the ball and use that final pause as a last-minute checkup. But the moment I start that club head back, I stick to my decision. Indecision now is fatal.

Whether you take a practice swing with your putter is a matter of individual taste. I rarely do. When I'm back of the ball, I finger the putter grip to sensitize my fingers. I also am getting the feel of the putter's weight in my hands.

Skee Riegel has a funny little practice swing. He lifts the putter above the ball and takes a tiny quarter-inch backswing and a half-inch follow-through. He does this whether he's got a 4-foot putt or a 40-footer. This obviously does something for him psychologically.

Others will take a practice swing over the ball to check their line of roll and the squareness of their putter. If any of these mannerisms help you, fine. My mannerism of setting myself pigeon-toed on long putts is probably only psychological.

But psychology is important in putting. If you find any trick that builds up your confidence, it is bound to reflect itself in better, more accurate putting.

But the best confidence-maker of all is to start dropping those 6-footers consistently and gaining the ability to lag those long ones up to a smaller and smaller radius of the cup.

One final practice pointer that has helped my game tremendously, particularly on short putts, is to use four tees. I place two tees, one a half inch off the toe of the putter; the other a half inch off the heel. Next, squarely on line of flight four inches behind, I place a second pair the same distance apart as the first two.

Now I practice my putting stroke, making sure the putter stays inside that "alley," on the backswing and on the stroke itself.

This is probably one of the best tests of whether your putter is square at all points during the stroke.

21

Thinking Your Way into the 80's

IN PLAYING OVER the years with amateurs, I have noticed a mistake common to most of them. Each one wants to hit the ball eight miles. They really want to belt it out of sight.

Perhaps their egotism offsets their good judgment. They remember the time they hit a given shot particularly well and got lots of distance; they forget that more often they don't do that well.

Also, I suspect that they want to keep up with the long-hitting pro and impress him by the distance of their shots.

Actually there is only one way you can impress a person on a golf course: that's by your score.

It isn't a question of how you played a particular shot, but a question of getting the ball to your objective. I don't care if you use a No. 2 iron, another member of the foursome takes a No. 4 iron, a third a No. 6, and the fourth a No. 7.

The only question is how many strokes you took on the hole, using whatever clubs you selected.

There is a natural tendency to try to match other players in your foursome, particularly on drives. If I'm teeing off first, I concentrate on one idea: I'm going to try to play within myself. I figure to drive the ball down the fairway where I know I can put it. There is a limit to how far I can drive, and I know my limitations.

Then when Mr. Long Ball Hitter gets up to the tee, I find something else to do. I pick out somebody in the gallery to look at, or some objective, or think about what I've already done on my own drive.

I simply divorce myself from sound, tone, everything about his tee shot. *I never watch him swing.* As a matter of fact I almost never watch another player drive.

For one thing, his drive may so belittle my efforts that I would start thinking about it if I paid attention to where he went. For another, I may start picking up his mistakes.

Yes, if you aren't careful you'll lose your own tempo. If there is a fast swinger in your crowd, you'll find that unconsciously you will start speeding up yourself.

If I were to watch anybody I'd watch Sam Snead or Ben Hogan. Some of their fine tempo sneaks into my game, and I start playing better because of it.

Both of these great players are particularly helpful. Each has a rhythm which is so smooth and so deliberate that often I find I'm hitting the ball stronger and farther when I watch either of them.

So if you play with someone whose tempo fits your swing, it may be all right to watch him. But I think most 90 shooters should usually deliberately train themselves *not* to watch anyone else. They should devote all their concentration to their own game.

If you feel that courtesy requires you to pay some attention to your golfing partners, pick out a spot on the fairway. Then, as the ball is hit, your eye will pick it up in flight.

There is another way to concentrate on your own game instead of the game of others in your foursome. If you are all about evenly matched, remind yourself that Mr. Long Ball Hitter has got to be losing strokes somewhere else in his game. Even if he is driving past you twenty-five or thirty yards, he isn't going to get his ball into the cup any faster than you— if you play your own game and play it well.

The temptation to watch your opponent is, I think, greatest in match play where each hole is a contest by itself. But even if those longer drives enable your opponent to win a few holes, your game, if you play consistently, will pay off in the long run.

Another frequent error made by most golfers is never to have enough club in their hands. They are always trying to hit an iron farther than it should be hit.

They invariably come up on the short side of the green.

Sometimes, of course, this should be done deliberately. If the pin is placed at the very back of the green, you should be short. If you are long in such a situation you have no point of return.

At the 18th at Tam O'Shanter, for example, if you put the ball over the end of the green, you're dead. You'd have to shoot it out of the grandstand. So you pick out a club that, at its maximum, will carry you to the flag.

Remember it is no disgrace to leave a ball just short of the green. Still, there is no excuse for being pathetically short, as amateurs so often are because they think they can hit a ball farther with a given club than they can. The remedy is quite simple: take one or two clubs more. If you are frequently hitting short with your No. 5 iron, for example, next time use a No. 4; or even a No. 3.

Another error of many 90 shooters is to rely too much on their caddy.

Some clubs have very fine professional caddies. I'll never forget the first time I played Pinehurst. I had a shot that looked like a No. 3 iron. The caddy recommended a No. 4 iron and I argued with him.

"Either you hit a No. 4 iron or I drop the bag and walk back to the clubhouse," he said.

He meant it too. And his judgment turned out to be correct.

I'll listen to a caddy and his advice about distance *if* he understands my game. But he'll have to know my finesse shots as well as my regular game. Unfortunately there aren't many caddies with that high degree of skill.

If I have a caddy with apparently sound judgment I may occasionally ask him what club to use. If he says a No. 7 and I've been debating about a No. 8, I'll at least have some basis for decision.

But I always make my own decision. You should too. To lean too heavily on your caddy is pure laziness. You should do your own thinking. Use your caddy only when you are sure he knows your game and then, only as a consultant; not as the person who makes up your mind for you.

As much as anything else, the difference between a 90 and an 80 shooter is a willingness to practice.

If you are able to play four or five times a week, you will be learning by playing. But that is a lot of golf for the average player. More likely he is lucky to get in two rounds a week.

He can, however, make up for this by planning a little practice session in his backyard. A fifteen- or twenty-minute warmup with a weighted club will do wonders for grooving your swing. Most driving ranges are open after dark to provide you another practice outlet.

It is important, however, to practice correctly. You aren't

just out there for the exercise. You are trying to improve your game.

I know of one young golfer who put himself in the hands of a good teaching pro. The first year he took up the game, he never went on the course. He spent the whole first season working on the practice tees and greens. Within two years he was the club champion.

Now few people will go to this extreme. After all, you are *playing golf, not working at it.* But this story does illustrate the benefits of practice, particularly to the golfer whose time on the course is limited.

The other ingredient for breaking through into the 80's is confidence.

I never start out a tournament with the idea of finishing tenth. I always figure I'm going to finish first. Obviously it doesn't work out that way every time. Sometimes, if it isn't my week, I'm satisfied with whatever I can make.

Perhaps you've wondered why younger pros seldom get into the money? The reason is lack of confidence and experience. They are afraid they won't qualify at the end of two rounds for the final 36-hole play-offs. They start worrying, and indecision sneaks into their game.

There are already enough tension moments on a golf course without adding needless worry to your list.

I worry about the problem at hand; not about qualifying for the final rounds. Usually I make it. If I don't, there's always next week and another tournament.

Sometimes I know I'm going to win. At least I will with breaks; and self-confidence helps create those breaks.

I also use psychology on myself. If I get a poor drive on the first hole, I always remind myself there are seventeen and a half holes left to rectify the error.

Everybody makes so many good shots in a round and so many bad ones. So, if you start out a little poorly, this may be a little upsetting, but after all it's a challenge. You've taken a bad shot or two; those are just so many bad ones out of your system.

Too many golfers have the trait of remembering too long what is already behind them. When a hole is over, it's over. If you have made a mistake, then the only thing the first hole can teach you is not to make that same mistake again. You'll make others, of course; but try not to repeat the same ones.

If I've bogeyed the first hole, I go to the second telling myself I can birdie this hole just as easily as I can par or bogey it. Then, if I do birdie it, I'm all even. That's just the same as starting with two pars.

However, all the psychology in the world won't help you if your game contains a fundamental weakness.

Review your game thoroughly and regularly. Try to pinpoint your problems, then seek out the cause of the error and correct it.

PART III

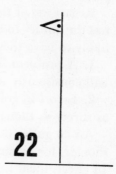

22

Getting into the 70's

A GOLFER WHO shoots in the 80's has the equipment to break par.

It is, of course, impossible to generalize about all 80 players. There are some who shoot well for 17 holes, then usually have one bad one.

There are others who play every club in their bag well, except one. That gives them trouble—and costs them strokes. Some will get jittery somewhere in the match and throw away strokes that they normally make with ease.

Still others have got into the 80's through natural ability, but remain there because they lack the patience to practice. They still go out on the golf course "cold" except for a few warm-up shots and throw away strokes until their game gets grooved.

Fortunately, however, most 80 shooters have a desire to improve and realize that the practice tee and green are as essential to a golf course as the 18 holes which they regularly play.

Regardless of the *details* of the problem, every player who has the ability to break par but who still shoots in the 80's is likely to have these faults:

1. A problem in his swing which prevents his hitting the ball consistently where he wants it to go.

2. Errors in golfing judgment that throw away strokes just as surely as though he had dubbed a shot.

An 80 golfer doesn't have much margin for error. An 85 shooter, for example, is only thirteen strokes over a par 72. In effect, then, he has made only thirteen errors in a round (fifteen if he birdies a couple of holes).

Viewed another way, if the 85 shooter eliminates thirteen bad strokes from his game, he is automatically a par shooter.

Sounds simple, the skeptic might say, *too* simple.

But, having played with hundreds of 80 golfers in pro-amateur tournaments, I am convinced that at least half of their extra strokes can be eliminated by making a change in their style of play. The other half are errors in judgment which can be overcome with good golf thinking right now.

The player who shoots in the 80's should first analyze his own game by taking the score cards of his last three or four rounds. First of all, is there any pattern to his scoring? Is there one hole which is causing most of the trouble?

If so, what's the reason? Sometimes, of course, it is psychological. Because you've done poorly on that hole before, you lack confidence in your ability to master it.

But often it is a case of bad judgment; of stubbornly playing the hole the same way time and time again. The obvious answer is to restudy the problems on that given hole to see if there isn't another, a better, way to play it.

If your problem doesn't simplify down to one hole, then let's take another look at the score card. Were there any double-bogeys and why? Usually these come when you hit an out-of-bounds shot or hit into the rough, losing an extra stroke.

Three-putt greens, of course, will swell your score. You can't avoid an occasional three-putt green, but you certainly won't score well if you get too many.

Finally, does the score card give any hint of a weakness somewhere in your bag? Can you pin your problem on one club or one particular situation shot? If so, the practice tee is the answer clearly indicated.

Nearly all the possibilities that I have suggested looking for come under the category of mental errors or of failing to hit a consistent shot under various game conditions.

You have now reached the stage in your golfing development where merely hitting a ball isn't enough. Nor is it enough to get distance on your drives and fairway shots.

Now your improvement must come in *placing* your shots for maximum accuracy. Let me show you how.

23

The "Champion's Grip"

PROFESSIONAL TEACHING says that the V's of both hands should point to the right shoulder. This is the strongest position for the hands. Therefore, it is the grip which should be used by the high-handicap player and the beginner.

However, as your game improves, this grip might result in a consistent hook. Nearly every player who shoots in the low 80's and high 70's has been, in my experience, a hooker and a pronounced hooker on occasions.

When I first broke into the pro ranks in 1949, I was a strong hooker. Too many times I would hit a very wicked hook and the ball would go out of bounds.

Well, if you hope to get into the money in pro ranks, you can't be throwing away shots on out-of-bounds hooks. You also can't lose strokes by hooking a ball so badly you get into heavy rough and have to waste a shot recovering.

Lack of perfect control of the ball can cost you strokes too. Let me give you a simple example. If you put your

146

second fairway shot where you want it, you have an easy 5-iron to the green. But if your second shot isn't right, you leave yourself a *tough* 5-iron shot. And since the law of averages says you'll miss more of the tough ones than the easy ones, that, simply, means more strokes.

In tournament play such errors mean finishing among the also-rans. To the 80 player they spell failure to his hope of getting down into the low 70's.

In addition to getting rid of my troublesome hook, therefore, I wanted a ball I could always control.

My first step was to get rid of that hook and turn my ball into a very slight fade, so I began to experiment with my grip.

Gradually I moved my hands around the club, taking various positions. Some golfers have even gone so far as to experiment with a grip having the V's pointing toward the left, but this proves to be too extreme for most of us.

The grip I settled on has the V's pointing to my chin. It is still the same palm grip in the left hand, finger grip in the right. The only difference is in the position of the V's. Instead of pointing toward the inside of my right shoulder, they point to my chin.

This grip has a great many effects on your swing. At first it may produce an occasional bad slice. You've got to spend time working on it until you eliminate that danger. But eventually it will produce a more dependable swing.

This new hand position has a major effect on your hand action too. By placing the hands on top of the club, the left becomes stronger. You do your hitting with the right; you guide with your left. When the V's are pointed over the right shoulder, the right hand has maximum strength and, sometimes overpowers the left. That is one cause of the bad hook.

With the V's pointed straight up, the left hand gains added power; the right loses some. Now it is harder for the right hand to overpower the left, and you will seldom throw the swing out of its orbit.

This "champion's grip" takes something off your shots. In the old days I used to belt a ball out 250 yards; today my average is closer to 230. But it is an accurate 230 instead of a maybe-good, maybe-bad 250.

I mention this because some golfers hesitate to lose distance, particularly on their drives. Yet if there is one place where distance should be at a premium it is on the tournament circuit. There are tournament courses where the long-ball hitter can win because wide fairways and easy rough and traps aren't much of a handicap for a shot that goes wild.

But when it comes to the big ones—the Masters, the National Open, the PGA and the two Tam O'Shanter tournaments—good accurate golf is needed not only to win but to finish up among the leaders.

Even when I was belting them, I wasn't the longest hitter on the course by any means. Yet it was only after I took something off my drives and substituted accuracy that I started winning.

Whether my grip will work for you is something you'll have to find out yourself. Most women golfers and men whose hands are not particularly strong would probably have trouble with it. Certainly anyone with a tendency to slice ought not to experiment with it at all.

But the chronic hooker should try it by all means and this covers a large percentage of the 80 shooters.

In this book I've mentioned several times the value of the weighted practice club. Any time I want to fool around with my grip, I take out my practice club and swing it for ten or fifteen minutes. In that time you can almost form a new grip.

At first this grip may not seem as comfortable as your old grip—and there's a reason. You've taken away some of that right-hand power to which you are accustomed.

I wouldn't advise you to change abruptly from a V's-to-the-

right to the upright V's position. Do your own experimenting until you find the hand position that eliminates your bad
hook. Eventually you too may settle on the upright V position; but the mere process of experimenting will help you.

For one thing you'll learn confidence in your new grip
because you've practiced it enough to know how and why
it works. For another it won't raise undue complications
with the rest of your game if you let yourself gradually make
the needed adjustments.

Even though I have settled on my grip I recheck it periodically. The only time I have trouble now with a severe hook
is when my left hand begins to creep over. So when I find
a hook has started to work its way into my game, I spend time
with my practice club and on the practice tee—devoting my
entire time to my grip.

When I form my grip my left hand sits pretty much on
top of the shaft, my thumb is just slightly to the right. But,
in general, my grip is just about straight up and down the
shaft. The back of my left hand is square to the proposed
line of flight.

This grip also changes the position of the hands and club
head at the top of the backswing. With the V's to the right,
your left hand is cocked at the top of the backswing so that
there is a crease at the wrists.

When you point the V's upright, the left hand remains
straight. If you'll look at the picture in the endpapers showing my position at the top of the backswing, you will note
that my arm and hand are straight from shoulder to knuckles,
the club face is in a square position.

Throughout the book until now I have stressed the "inside-out" swing. The high-handicap player can visualize the
arc of the swing better if he "sees" it as a swing in which the
club head cuts slightly across the ball in an outward angle.

My good friend, Ron La Parl, who is the pro at the Battle
Creek (Michigan) Country Club, was one of the first teach-

ing pros to start giving his better pupils the new concept
which top pros employ in their swing.

Ron, in addition to being a first-rate instructor, spends
part of his winter on the tournament circuit, so he knows
both amateur and professional styles well.

My swing, and that of the top pros, isn't an inside-out
swing at all. It is actually an "inside-inside" swing. Our club
head never gets out beyond the proposed line of flight except for a "cut" shot. The top pro takes his club head back
inside, strikes the ball, and keeps his club *inside* on the
follow-through.

I have a very upright swing. That's because I stand up
quite straight to the ball, and naturally the straighter you
stand at address, the more upright your swing will be.

One difficulty with the upright swing is that you always
have the tendency, or at least the sensation, of falling forward. From time to time, as I've said before, I conscientiously try to flatten out my own swing. The more your
weight is back on your heels at address and backswing, the
lower your plane becomes and the flatter your swing. This in
turn keeps your shoulders more parallel and averts one of my
problems, a tendency to dip my left shoulder.

But, even though I practice a flatter swing, I find myself
playing pretty much upright in tournaments. So, just like
yourself, I have my golfing problems. Real golfing perfection
is always just around the corner, but you spend a lifetime at
the game hunting for it.

But, whether he swings upright or has a flat swing (or,
usually preferable, something in between), the good golfer
stays with his shot. After my club head strikes the ball, it
follows after the ball along the proposed line of flight for a
good foot or foot and a half. If you took the arc of my swing,
you would find that the follow-through stays low to the
ground much longer than the period immediately preceding the striking of the ball.

In other words, the angle of the arc of my swing *into the ball is fairly sharp; the follow-through is a more sweeping action*. It is almost as if the ball were stuck to the club head for about 18 inches and I was making sure the club face propelled the ball toward the target.

No golfer, of course, *consciously* follows through. The follow-through is a direct result of what went before—the backswing and the downswing through the ball.

The longer arc of the follow-through comes because I've got my left side out of the way at impact and the centrifical force of my swing has carried the club head on past the point of impact.

After the club head starts to rise naturally on the follow-through, my wrists carry it on through until my hands naturally turn over and I wind up with a good finish to my swing.

When I tee off, I pick some object to aim for. So when I hit through the ball, I want the club head to be aiming for that target.

Many of the top pros today play a ball with a slight fade. However, Bobby Locke and others prefer the right-to-left, slightly hooking motion.

In my case I want the ball to rise rapidly, reach its peak, and then descend with a feathery, floating action which I achieve by a slight fade.

I find this gives me maximum accuracy. It is a little easier for me to visualize the flight of the ball when it has this left-to-right flight. The softer descent of the ball also means that it will have less roll, and I have much less trouble with a bad bounce, or with the shot that keeps going after it hits and rolls on into trouble.

I used to hit the ball harder and produced a low-flying ball. On some greens I'd be all right. I was safest, of course, when they were wet and had plenty of "stick" to them. But on hard, fast greens I was getting into trouble.

Where formerly the ball would take maybe fifteen feet

before it started to "bite," now I found it coming in like a feather. So, providing I had a good lie, I could afford to throw the ball at the flag and not worry about it.

I get that high floating shot with the slight left-to-right flight by a sawing action.

I take my regular swing, but get my left side out of the way faster. This, in effect, turns my body more toward the target at impact; in turn producing a "sawing" action of the club head "under" the ball.

Opening the club face provides the other feature of the flight of the ball—the high, feathery flight. I only open the club face a trifle for most shots. You can increase the height of your shot when you need to by opening it still farther.

One check, of course, is the divot. With the cut shot it goes across the line and slightly inside the line of flight.

Under normal circumstances I cut every shot. But I want to emphasize the fact that the left-to-right action is very slight. When I'm hitting the ball well, it almost appears to be flying perfectly straight—the fade is that delicate. Occasionally, if my timing is off, I will run into a bad slice. But usually this can be remedied by hitting a few practice balls.

One other point should be emphasized. My grip and the arc of my swing are designed for only one purpose: to erase a bad hook and to increase my accuracy. If, after you have given this method a fair trial, it doesn't work for you (it won't for everybody), abandon it.

A slightly open stance with the regular grip is sometimes enough to eliminate a bad hook and produce a "controllable" ball.

But now you've reached the stage of golfing know-how where you can not only afford to experiment with your game, but must do so if you want to keep improving your score. But experiment wisely. Just because a given method works for me isn't a guarantee that it will work for you as well.

Now once again remember that this new grip may produce a slice—sometimes a bad one. With practice it should straighten out to a slight fade. If it doesn't, forget it.

Accuracy is your goal. Experiment until you find the swing that is right for you.

24

Getting More Distance

Most GOLFERS, including many professionals, have poor footwork. This costs them distance because golfing power comes from the ground up. If your footwork is poor, your hips and shoulders won't work right, and you lose all the momentum of body power in your swing.

Some teaching pros advocate an absolute transfer of weight from the left to the right foot on the backswing. This is an effort to help the golfers who persist in keeping their weight concentrated on their left side. However, an artificial transfer of weight is likely to give you the lateral movement we are guarding against.

If you look at sequence pictures of any top professional, you will immediately spot the fact that his feet are "alive." They are not planted in static fashion through the hitting area. They are giving him balance and power.

Take a look at the sequence pictures on the endpapers of this book, which show my swing with a No. 4 iron.

Note first the right leg from the position of address to the top of the backswing. You will see that it doesn't move—it is a stationary, firm foundation to my swing.

The knee is bent slightly inward. That is because my weight is on the *inside* spikes of my right foot. In a sense I am pivoting *against* that muscular barrier of the instep and the inside of my right thigh.

My body can't sway to the right because the barrier prevents it.

Now take a look at my left foot and leg in the back swing. There is a slight blur from my trouser cuff that obscures a bit of the left-foot action. But you will note that my left knee is also slightly bent inward at address, as is my right. My weight is back toward my heels and on the inside spikes of both feet.

As the club head goes back, my left foot rolls over on the instep, but the heel never leaves the ground. At the top of my backswing, my weight is on both insteps, just as it was at address.

The only difference is that where my weight was evenly divided at address, now it is more on my right side—something like a 60-40 distribution.

Next see what happens as I start the club head down. My left foot returns firmly to the ground as I get my left side out of the way of my swing.

I have a "pushing" sensation with the ball of my right foot as I come into the hitting area. Some pros will get that pushing sensation from all of the inside spikes of their right foot and the right heel remains on the ground.

You will note that I've almost got my right toes digging into the ground.

At impact and follow through my momentum is such that my left foot rolls over to where the weight is now on the *outside* spikes of my left foot.

In the later stages of my follow through, you will see that

the body turn is unrestricted and it pulls my right foot around, but my right toes are still digging into the ground.

My head remains stationary throughout the entire swing until the natural turning motion of my body pulls it up in the follow-through.

Finally note that my left arm remains straight from address, through the backswing and downswing, until I am well into my follow-through.

There you have three factors which remain unchanged—the head steady, the left arm straight and the inside of the right leg forming a barrier against a lateral shift of the body.

I'd like you to pay particular attention to the opening movements of the backswing. You can see how the club head is swung back in a compact, one-piece swing.

The turn of the hips and shoulders and the cocking of the wrists are all shown in the subsequent pictures. The pictures following clearly illustrate the "coiled" feeling I get at the very top.

The very next picture showing the start of the downswing catches the proper movement perfectly. You will notice that the downswing has been started by the hips; nothing else has moved. The hips become square very quickly and this, and this alone, has caused the club head to move downward.

With the hip turn, the weight is shifting to the left side, from the inside to the outside of my left foot.

See how quickly that weight shift has taken place. My weight is largely on my left side while my hands are still waist high.

The hips keep turning. This is the sensation I described as "getting my left side out of the way quickly."

I'd like you to pay particular attention to my hands in the downswing. You will see that they remain fully cocked until they are down around my hips; my shoulders are square and my hips are turned slightly open. At this point the forward pressure on my right instep is acting as a catalyst to maximum club-head speed and power. Then I really "pour it on" through the hitting area.

Check the picture which immediately follows the point of impact and note how low the club head is. This is what I meant when I said to stay with the ball after contact. The club head is "following" the ball toward the target.

At this point my weight is on the outside of my left foot and this serves as a barrier, just as the firm right side did in the backswing.

You will note that the hands and left arm remain square until my hands are about even with my left hip, then they gradually "roll" over as I keep my arms straight right on through to the top of the follow through.

The final stage of the swing shows me facing the hole; the last movement coming as my right foot pivots on the toes to bring me around for the "picture finish" of the golf swing.

If you have a motion-picture camera available, you may find it of great value to take movies of your own swing and compare it with these shots of mine. I have used a camera in some of my teaching and I find it extremely helpful because the pictures quickly show a golfer where he is losing power.

Timing is all-important in golf. Compare the pictures of the backswing and downswing, matching them up by noting the position of the club head.

You will note that many of the pictures look almost like duplicates. The difference is in the foot action and in the hips. On the downswing the hips have turned, and the weight is moving to the left side.

Notice also that it takes three frames of the sequence pictures to show my club head moving back just a few feet, but only one to show the club head hitting through the same area on the downswing. This gives a graphic demonstration of the speed of the club head in the hitting area.

If footwork is your problem, take out your weighted club

and swing it back and forth through three or four swings without stopping. Pay attention to your feet as you do this and learn the "feel" of active footwork.

Translated into your golf game, active footwork means more power and distance.

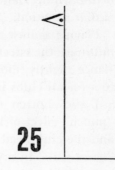

25

"Finesse" Shots for the Better Golfer

IF EVERY DAY were perfect, with no wind and no rain, if every fairway and green were always in top shape, and if your ball always stayed on the fairway, golf would be a much simpler game.

But, of course, it doesn't work out that way. You are bound to hit shots into the rough now and then. And rain and wind will change a golf course from one day to the next.

That's the reason the pro has his "finesse" shots—the professional secrets you need to take off strokes you couldn't save with a normal shot.

First, let's take a common problem—playing on a day when the wind is blowing.

One problem with wind is that it tends to upset your balance and timing. When I play with the wind behind me, the club head feels heavier on the backswing. To overcome this I widen my stance just a trifle.

With the wind behind me, the ball will travel farther, so

159

I cut down by one or two clubs depending on the velocity of the wind. I also play the ball more forward in this particular situation.

Playing against the wind, you want a low-traveling ball to minimize the effect of the wind. At such times I narrow my stance slightly, move the ball back a trifle toward my right foot for all clubs including the woods.

I also shorten my backswing somewhat to increase the "punch" effect of keeping my hands ahead of the club head and the club head low on the follow through. And I want "more club" in my hand to make up for lost distance.

For example, where the shot might normally be a No. 5 iron, I would take either a No. 4 or a gripped-down No. 3.

Whenever I want to play a punch shot because I'm not positive of the distance, I'm a great advocate of the gripped-down shot. Normally, as you know, I leave a half-inch of the grip exposed above my left hand. To grip down, I move my hands down another inch or so. Then I take a very easy three-quarters swing.

This gripped-down shot gives you confidence. You *know* you have enough club in your hands and you aren't tempted to belt the ball. Instead you try to "finesse" it to your objective.

Many golfers fail to note how hard the wind is blowing and in what direction. If there's any doubt in your mind of the strength and direction of the wind, throw some dry grass into the air. And also check the trees and the flag. Sometimes there will be fairly strong wind from where you are shooting, but around the green it will be either blocked out by the tall trees or channeled into a slight cross-wind.

So, don't just check the wind from where you are shooting, but visualize the flight of your ball and check the wind conditions affecting its flight later on.

Some days, however, the wind is puffy. There isn't any set rule for playing under these conditions except to urge you to be extremely careful in your club selection. And in all types of wind keep your swing smooth and, above all, *when you are shooting into it don't try to fight it by overpowering the ball.*

Where you are playing into a cross-wind, you usually will need one more club because the wind will take something off your shot. The average player should take a cross-wind into account in aiming the ball either to the right or the left of his objective.

However, as you get into the low-handicap category you can afford to experiment with a slight fade or hook into the wind. As a matter of fact I like to play on a day with a light breeze blowing because the breeze acts as a sort of backstop for my left-to-right or right-to-left shots.

But in a stronger cross-wind, most players fare better if they play their regular game and allow for the wind to carry the ball to the right or the left.

Another common weather problem is rain. Under these conditions make sure that your club face is striking the ball sharply. Otherwise the dampness on the ball and club face may produce a skidding shot.

In bad lies, especially in clover, I try to hood the club face slightly because hitting in wet clover is like hitting in grease.

And then there are the times when your ball lands in a fairway bunker with a lot of distance left to the green. What I do then depends on the bunker. If there is a low lip, I take a gripped-down No. 4 wood.

Bury your feet so that you get a good foundation; then swing firmly at the ball, always making sure to hit it cleanly. Here especially you must avoid trying to overpower the ball. A smooth swing is essential.

If you have a bad lie, there is, of course, only one thing to do: get your ball out of the trap with an explosion.

Water is primarily a mental hazard, but it must also figure in your strategy.

If you are a low-handicap player and can clear a water hazard with a fine shot—not necessarily a perfect shot—then go ahead and try it. But, if you are in any doubt, play safe.

Further, if shooting over water makes you nervous, take a club or two more. You've probably got a club in your bag which will certainly clear the obstacle. If you haven't, play safe.

Sometimes you want to throw an extra-soft shot up to the green. In this instance, instead of using a pitching wedge, I suggest you choose a sand wedge. It produces a higher, softer shot.

When I'm shooting for a hard green on a short par 3, I'll tee the ball up purposely a little higher than usual. With the ball teed up at normal height, it would strike the "sweet spot" of the blade. By teeing higher, you strike the ball higher up on the club face. This costs you some distance, but produces a higher, "deader" ball when it hits.

By now, if you've followed each step of the book, you know something about hooking or fading a ball. There are times when you must deliberately fade or hook to get your ball around an obstacle, such as a tree.

To get a deliberate, severe hook, I close my stance and move my left hand to a stronger position so that the V of my left hand will now point toward the inside of my right shoulder.

I take the club head back in a normal swing. But on the downswing I bring my hands back so that the V's at impact are pointing toward my chin. This produces a slight rolling action to the wrists and closes the club face at impact.

I control the amount of hook by how far I turn the V's to the right.

For a deliberate slice, I open the club face and take a more open stance and concentrate on an outside-in arc to my swing. By adjusting the degree from my normal position that I open my stance, I determine the amount of fade I put on the ball.

These tips should prove handy at least several times during an average round. They will help cut off several strokes on your way to par golf.

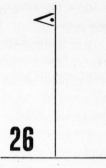

26

Playing the Dog-Leg Holes

As EVERY GOLFER knows, there are two types of dog-leg holes—one curves off to the left, and the other curves off to the right. Either type presents extra golfing problems.

On such problem holes I go by "instinct." If there is a choice between using a driver or a safer club I decide on the basis of how I have been playing up to that point.

If I've been driving well that day, I'll consider the driver. Then I must be sure that I am confident enough to stand on the tee without "freezing." If I have figured out that I can make the required shot with the driver, I may go at it. A No. 1 wood will gain me a little distance and shorten a bit my second shot to the green.

But if there is any doubt in my mind whether I can execute the shot correctly, then I have to figure out how to get almost the same results by being a little more conservative. I want to be sure I am choosing the best percentage shot.

164

Consider the problem when you are playing a 450-yard hole with a bunker on your left.

Well, the first thing you decide is that your tee shot might hit that bunker.

But since this is dog-leg to the left, the bunker "guards" the short way to the green.

I generally follow the old pro rule of teeing up on the side of trouble. So now I'll tee up on the left side, which will make me shoot out more to the right.

I'll pick a target so many yards to the right of that bunker and aim for it.

I'm assuming that the bunker is set so that I can't carry it with my driver, or, at best, not by much. I'll aim then roughly for the middle of the fairway.

If I make a serious error, the worst that can happen is that I'll find myself out in the light rough on the right side of the fairway. Nevertheless I have succeeded in keeping away from that bunker.

If I hit an exceptionally good tee shot, I'll have an easier second shot. But if I err slightly, I'll have only a slightly tougher second shot. Even a bad error will still leave me with a good chance to get my second on the green.

Usually if I've taken a "conservative" tee shot, I can't go for the pin. This is a hole you will rarely birdie unless you come up with one of those miraculous second shots. I'm content to reach the green in two and settle for my par with two putts.

Now let's consider the same problem where the bunker is close enough so that your tee shot will clear the obstacle if you hit it well but not quite perfectly. Again ask yourself how confident you really are of clearing that obstacle if you hit something less than a perfect shot. If you're convinced that the gamble is in your favor, go ahead and try it.

Whether you play 100 golf or shoot a sub-par round as a

pro, the principle remains the same: figure the odds and let them favor *you* on every golfing decision you make.

Sometimes, of course, those gambles don't work out because that every-once-in-a-while trouble creeps into your game. When that happens I can't help it any more than you can. All I ask is that the percentages be in my favor. When they are, and I goof, that's just one of the breaks in the game over which I had no control.

A second dog-leg that you'll find on most courses is one in which the "turn" is guarded by tall trees. Let's say that this is a dog-leg right.

Here we must decide whether to fade the ball or hit it straightaway. Naturally, because the green is off to the right, we'll tee off on that side and we'll try to play the ball to the left or out straight as far as possible.

Now if you hit a bad drive you're going to be in the rough, but if you cut that dog-leg close you aren't going to get the ball out far enough. Your next shot will be blocked by the trees.

So, basically you will be better off *across the fairway*. From there your second shot will be to an open green because the very angle of your tee shot will "open up" the green for you.

Every hole, of course, is different, and you've got to know the characteristics of the particular hole you're playing.

But, regardless of the details, you should always ask yourself these questions:

1. If I miss my shot, how far will I miss it?
2. Will the ball still have trees blocking my path to the green?
3. Will even a missed shot get me around the corner?

You don't try to pull off a spectacular shot, because the percentages are against you.

There is another factor you must consider in playing dog-legs. That is, how you're hitting the ball. If you are a consistent hooker or consistent slicer, you have to figure out how to play such holes by visualizing the path your ball is going to take.

Unfortunately everybody's game isn't consistent day-in and day-out. One reason for going out to the practice tee in advance is to find out just how you are playing on that particular day.

Perhaps your right hand is strong today and you are hooking the ball. Or you may be fading the ball a bit more than normally.

After you practice for a while, you'll determine whether you're hitting left-to-right, or right-to-left. Usually you can't fight the way your game shapes up on a given day.

I naturally fade the ball slightly. But sometimes I get more fade than usual. That's the reason I use the practice tee to find out just how I am hitting the ball on that particular day.

I remember one round in the Goodall tournament. Fred Hawkins, Ed Furgol, and Ben Hogan made up my foursome. We came to the par 5 sixth hole, and Ben had an exacting spoon shot. He was dead center on his tee shot. The green was guarded both right and left by deep bunkers.

The fade shot is Ben's specialty. But, for some reason the ball didn't fade this time, and he hit it squarely well to the left of the left bunker, getting down in five for his par and losing three points to his opponents.

On the ninth hole an identical situation arose; again he failed to put fade on the ball. You could almost bet your bankroll that Hogan wouldn't miss that particular shot twice in a row. However, this cost him a double bogey and more points.

The 16th hole was another par 5 and it took a good spoon to get home in two. Unbelievably, for the third time, Ben pulled his shot. He is usually calm, at least outwardly. But he promptly took that spoon and pounded it on the ground with a fair amount of head speed.

So you see even for one of the all-time greats, there can be days in which the most reliable shot goes sour. Now I would have done the same thing as Hogan; I would have tried to fade that third shot. After all, we've hit the ball that way hundreds of times. It doesn't stand to reason that either of us would hit a third such shot badly in one round.

But it *can* happen. So when I find a given club going sour, I tend to shy away from it whenever I have an alternative. On the other hand, when I find I'm hot with a given club I'll favor it.

But once the round is over, there is only one thing to do. That is to take the guilty club out on the practice tee and find out what's causing the trouble.

Once you've determined how you're playing, through the practice tee and early holes and come to the dog-leg problem, apply these rules:

1. Do what you know you can do.

2. Don't try to do the impossible or gamble on the "perfect" shot.

3. When you decide what you *may* be able to do, weigh the alternatives—what trouble you are in if you miss, what advantage you gain if you make it.

4. Make your decision and go to it.

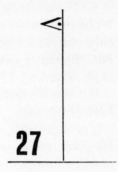

The "Advanced" Bunker Shot

ONE OF THE FINESSE shots that I deliberately left out of chapter 25 was the advanced bunker shot.

Until you have experience, you should only try to get the ball out of the trap. The higher-handicap player will have all he can do to learn not to "press" in a trap and wind up taking extra strokes.

If, however, you have now reached the stage where you have confidence (and the scores to prove it) that you can get out of a bunker consistently, then you're ready for the next step.

If you come out with a single explosion shot, but leave yourself a long chip or a long approach putt, you'll seldom get down in par.

So the next step is to learn to "control" your explosion shot.

There are three factors to consider:

1. Where the ball lies

2. The type of sand

3. The distance from the bunker to the cup

If you have an exceptionally good lie, you may be able to chip out. If a bunker has no lip, occasionally you can putt out. In either case, simply apply the methods we have already discussed.

If your lie demands an explosion shot, aim a half inch back of the ball.

The same rule applies where the ball is partially buried. However, the distance that you aim behind the ball will depend on how badly it is buried.

I have encouraged you to keep a smooth, even, unhurried tempo in a sand trap. This rule will apply to all sand-trap shots, including one where the sand is wet, or packed down, or coarse.

If there is any doubt of the consistency of the sand, test it as you dig your feet in at your address and act accordingly.

Next, let's discuss the question of distance.

I am assuming now that you can not only get the ball out of the trap, but that you are able to hit it *on the line* toward the cup. If you aren't doing this every time, you are not properly lined up toward your target.

Now there are several ways in which the pros control distance. Some do it by the tempo of their swing. Still others hit closer to the ball for maximum distance, farther back (thus taking more sand) for less distance.

The method I use is extremely simple and has proved very effective for me. I like to play all my shots, except under unusual circumstances, off the left instep. To move the ball around just seems to be adding an extra headache. So trying to gauge distance by how far behind the ball I hit doesn't feel right.

Nor do I like to rely on a change of tempo. I prefer to use the same reliable even tempo for all my bunker shots.

My solution is to employ the technique that I use with

"cut" shots off the fairway or rough. For, say, a 15-foot explosion shot I'll open the blade just slightly. To cut down distance I'll open the blade more. With experience, I have learned how much to open the blade to get the required distance.

That's all there is to it.

Try it yourself. Just make sure that as you open the blade, you take your proper open stance *and be sure the edge of the blade is square to the proposed line of flight to the cup.*

As you perfect this finesse bunker shot, you'll be improving your scores because you'll be laying the ball up to the cup with the same assurance you would chip from off the green.

28

Practice Makes Perfect

MY ADVICE to 80 golfers who want to get into the 70's may be stated in one word: practice.

You've got to get out and practice every day until each shot becomes as much a part of your game as lacing up your golf shoes. A daily practice session with a weighted club will help you to groove your swing.

However, you must also spend more time on the practice tee.

When I go out to practice I take a whole bag of balls and go through it several times. That means a hundred or so practice shots.

I start out with my short irons and gradually work my way up to my driver. I consider every practice shot as important as though a tournament relied on playing it right. I also use the practice time to check my grip, my stance, my timing—all the details of my swing. If I'm having trouble with a given shot or a given club, I use my practice sessions to find out why—and correct the fault.

Yet merely practicing isn't enough. There must be purpose and reason behind your efforts.

You can't expect to pick up all the pointers I have covered in this section of the book by spending a few sessions on the practice tee.

But in large measure your progress from the 80's to the 70's will be rapid or slow depending upon the time you are willing to spend in *learning better golf through practice*.

You cannot expect to break 80 consistently until you swing consistently. Practice is the only way to acquire a grooved, reliable swing.

You can profit by analyzing your game. Hitting a "pretty good" shot isn't enough any more. You've got to learn to hit each shot in the bag with increasing accuracy, to cut down gradually the number of times a given shot goes "sour."

Take stock of your game periodically to spot any weak points; then practice until they become strong points.

Your short game especially must be reliable. Allow some time in each practice session for chipping and approaching; and, above all, take time on the practice green to polish up your putting.

Then, when you go out to play a round, keep learning. Put into practice what you have learned. As your technique improves, so will your confidence; and improved confidence marks the path to par golf.

PART IV

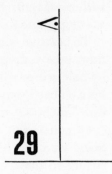

29

How to Shoot Par Golf

Once you break 80 consistently, you are ready to bring your score down to par figures. However, cutting strokes now is no easy task.

As a 78 shooter, for example, you have much of the technical skill needed in first-rate golf. You are just a step away from having complete control over your clubs.

But that "short step" means you've probably hit two shots out of bounds or into the kind of rough where you are bound to waste a stroke or two. You've made a few birdies, but you've probably had three three-putt greens.

On some of those bad greens most likely you left yourself 20-footers instead of short tap-in putts after your approaches, chips, or bunker shots.

Most of the top scorers in any professional tournament hit well from tee to green. The sub-par golfer is hot with his putter and his short game must be especially sharp.

Occasionally, of course, a scrambler gets up among the

money winners. He always seems to be in the sand traps, but still scores well. He is generally an artist with his sand wedge to compensate for his less dependable long game.

To analyze exactly how you yourself are playing right now, take your past several rounds and compare your hole-by-hole scores with par. Even the top pros rarely par every hole. They'll have some birdies and some bogeys to balance up. The hotter they are, of course, the fewer the bogeys.

Of course not all holes of the same par are equally easy. Some we call "birdie" holes because they give us the best chance to shave a stroke off par; on others we have to fight to get par and a slight error means a bogey.

One way to figure out *your* scoring is to take the handicap rating assigned to each hole on your course. Are you getting your pars on the "easier" holes? If you aren't, you'd better find out why, because, if you're playing percentage golf, these are the holes you should master first.

What holes have you bogeyed, and why, the last few times you've played?

Are you hitting all the fairways on your drives? Remember every shot out of the rough cuts down your percentage of reaching the green in two under par.

Are you positioning your drives and second shots properly? Or are you losing strokes because you're obliged to try the harder second or third shots?

Finally, are you three-putting the greens?

If you are missing the fairways with your drives you need work in that department. Too many golfers press for extra yardage on their drives and get a bad hook or slice as a result. You may be guilty of this if you are scoring poorly on the long par 4's or par 5's.

Now we all make a certain number of mistakes on the golf course. There are times when even the best golf swing comes "unglued." This usually happens when we find ourselves in a spot where we have to gamble and we try a little too hard. Such errors can't be helped.

But we can avoid errors caused by poor gambling. Make sure you aren't still losing strokes by attempting shots where the percentages are tilted too much against you.

Errors in strategy can also be avoided. The mark of a professional is his ability to think one shot ahead. He is concerned with where each shot will land in terms of the shot that follows.

From a distance he'll be alert to the "entrance" to the green. As he gets closer he'll be concerned with the contours of the green, the traps, the pin position. He's always trying to make his next shot as easy as possible.

It is a good idea for the 78 shooter to think of his game in two parts: first, his drive and (on par 5's) his second fairway shot, and second, everything that happens from the spot where he can reach the green until his ball drops into the cup.

The first part, driving and fairway shots, should be, plainly enough, aimed at keeping the ball in play on the fairway and getting it to the spot where the shot to the green has the best chance of succeeding.

On long approach shots, I aim for the center of the green and rely on my putting. On the shorter approaches, I go for the pin if I can safely do so, thus cutting down my putting problems.

But *always learn by your mistakes*. Why did the ball fall short of the green? Why did it go into the bunker? Sometimes you had bad luck, but many times the shot before was not played properly. Find out why.

Just reaching the green in two under par isn't good enough, either, if you leave the ball at the far end of the green where you have an extremely long approach putt.

Now whenever you shoot for the center of the green on a long approach and hit reasonably close, that's fine. But if you're aiming for the center and the ball isn't "holding" or is way off line, you've got to spot the trouble quick or you'll soon be missing the greens altogether.

Most of the strokes separating the 78 shooter from par have to be eliminated through playing experience. But many are directly traceable to a slight error in your swing that only practice will cure. No golfer can ever neglect his practice work on the tee and greens and expect his game to stay consistently good.

The other ingredient of par golf is concentration—the ability to play one shot at a time. That's the mark of champions. We'll discuss it next.

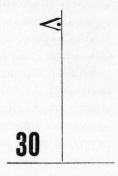

30

Thinking Like a Pro

As you perfect your swing, you gradually edge your score down to par figures. Skill plays its role; but so do judgment, strategy, and planning your game.

To help you think like a pro let's take a playing lesson. Come along with me as I played my two big ones of 1957—the National Open and the Tam "World." I'll reconstruct those matches, tell you why I played certain holes as I did, and try to point out along the way how to relate this kind of thinking to your own game.

The '57 Open was held at Inverness in Toledo, Ohio. On this, as on any Open course, they've toughened it up. There are new bunkers and a lot of heavy rough. The fairways are narrow.

So you must drive accurately to set yourself up for an easier second shot. If you're in the rough all day, you'll have a hard time getting anywhere near par.

In an Open the pros figure that par will generally win.

Ben Hogan had a four-under 276 at Riviera in 1948, but that was an exception to the rule.

On the four rounds I aimed to shoot par 280, or as close to it as I could. I was playing conservatively, and I gambled only when I was reasonably sure of the outcome.

I didn't want to throw away any strokes. I wasn't trying to overpower the ball. I just wanted to keep it in play. Only when I was absolutely sure did I "let out" my drives.

As usual I planned to aim for the center of the green and depended upon my putting to take care of the pars. If I sank a long one, fine; but at least I always had a good chance for par on every hole.

Well, the first round worked out just about as I planned. I made a few bogeys and got a few birdies and I wound up with my par 70.

At the end of that first day I was confident that my shots were okay. I was driving well and I liked the course, which is always important psychologically in tournament play.

I went out on the second round with the same objective— to shoot par. Maybe this time, I hoped, I'd do even better because I'd analyzed the mistakes I'd made the first day and the second time around I hoped to correct them.

On the first day, for example, I got a bogey on the 17th by trying to use a driver. It was too tight a tee shot for a driver. The 17th is a slight dog-leg. If you didn't hook the ball or cut part of the rough on the left, you were in trouble. If you hit straightaway, you'd go into the rough on the opposite side.

So on the second round I hit a spoon (instead of a driver) because I knew I couldn't carry into that far-side rough. Where the ball landed I needed a No. 4 iron to reach the green instead of a No. 7 iron following a perfect drive.

But at least I had a perfect lie in a good spot where I could see the flag. Then I hit a fine iron and a good putt to pick up my birdie. That gave me confidence and I proceeded to birdie 18. The two birdies gave me a 68, two under par at the halfway point in the tournament.

As you know, the third and fourth rounds come on a Saturday—the rough one-day 36-hole grind.

In the morning I got my highest score—a 74—yet I played, I think, my best golf of the tournament. The reason I say this is because I hit all the greens and all the fairways except on the 17th hole. However, three three-putt greens, a bogey at the 17th, and no birdies raised my score to 74. On the 17th hole they had moved the tee back, so I was forced to take a driver. I hit a very bad drive which put the ball into extremely heavy rough, and then I needed a wedge to get back to the fairway.

Let me explain why I tackled this problem as I did.

After I reached my drive I walked on up ahead to look at the green. I decided that there was no way to get to it. If the ball had been in the same position on the fairway with a clear shot at the green, I would have used a No. 4 iron.

The rough was so tough that I felt I needed at least a No. 6 iron to get out. And obviously a No. 6 iron out of the rough wouldn't go as far as a No. 4 iron from the fairway.

Now, having decided I couldn't reach the green, my next problem was what could I do? There was a downhill fairway to the green.

Having selected a No. 6 iron as the minimum club to get me out of the rough, I tried to visualize where the shot would go. I figured that a No. 6 iron would wind up on the steep down slope about 60 yards short of the green.

Now what was my problem? The pin was very close to the front edge and right near a bunker on the left side. This looked like a pretty tight fit to go for on a downhill lie.

So the No. 6 iron didn't seem the right choice.

Next I tried to figure where a No 7 iron would land. It would also be on the down slope—but not much improvement.

A No. 9 iron, I thought, would put me right on top of the hill. It was level there, an almost perfect lie with no special problems. From there I would have a No. 8 or No. 9 iron to the green and I might be able to make a par 4 if I could get that shot close enough to the pin.

You must know when to gamble. This hole was no place to take unnecessary chances. The one thing I was trying to avoid was a double-bogey 6. Naturally I was trying to avoid a bogey 5 if I could, but I wanted to avoid a 6 by all means.

I decided my safest course was to place the ball on the hill-top. I pitched it out onto the fairway to that point. From there I hit a No. 9 iron—a shot I was pretty confident of making. The ball landed about 10 feet from the cup. I hit a good putt, but it didn't happen to drop, so I wound up with a bogey 5.

Here was a situation where gambling made no sense what-soever. It would have been foolhardy to try for the green after my tee shot. As it was, playing it as I did, I had a chance for a par. Actually I wound up with a bogey, but at least I avoided a double-bogey.

Going into the final round, I had a 212. Jimmy Demaret was leading by one stroke with 211 and Julius (Jay) Boros had 213.

Now I had two worries. One was catching up with Jimmy; the other was to make sure that while I was watching him, Jay didn't get hot and beat us both.

Cary Middlecoff was at 214. While he is one of the great-est competitors in golf, I was pretty sure he was out of it. If I beat Jimmy and Jay, I thought I would win.

At all golf tournaments it is hard to get any information on how your opponents are doing. Demaret had teed off a few hours ahead of me, and somewhere near the turn for home I heard that I was all even with him.

I birdied number 12, putting me a shot ahead. By now I

figured Demaret must have finished, but I had no idea of his score. The 13th is a par 3, an exacting hole with the pin up close to the front of the green, guarded by a bunker.

If your shot landed short of the green in the bunker, it was almost impossible to get down in two because of the pin placement. So I elected to play safe and shoot for the center of the green.

I landed 25 feet from the pin, which seemed like smart strategy. But I promptly proceeded to three-putt. (I had done the same thing in the morning, three-putting that green in the third round.) So I had apparently lost my shot back again to Demaret.

On the next few holes I was still in the dark. Nobody had broken through the ropes to give me the figures, and I didn't know what I had to do until I got to the 17th hole.

Then Lloyd Mangrum came up to me and said, "You know what you need to win, don't you?"

"I've got an idea I need par," I replied.

"You need two pars to tie Demaret and a par and a birdie to win," he answered.

Now I knew exactly what I had to do. I had to birdie either 17 or 18.

Number 17 is a dog-leg that's a drive and a No. 6 or No. 7 iron. I hooked my drive, not badly, but into the rough. I had a clear shot to the green. The ball was in the short rough, yet the lie was good.

The flag was close to the front of the green. If I went for it, that meant hitting a perfect No. 7 iron or I'd go into the bunker in front.

I finally figured that this was no place to gamble. I had the 18th coming up, which was a birdie hole. So I elected to play a No. 6 iron and aimed for the center of the green.

I put the ball about 20 feet above the hole, figuring maybe I could sink a birdie putt. It was a tough downhill one over a slick green. I thought I had canned it, but it just missed, and I tapped in the second one for a par.

Now I came to 18 with a par to tie; a birdie to win.

Three years before, I had the chance to win the Open on the 18th, but I blew my tee shot and the title. I determined then I would never make the same mistake again.

This time I was keyed up, but I knew exactly what I was doing. Where I had rushed ahead three years before, this time I let the gallery get set. I decided that even if I hit a bad shot, I'd give myself every chance.

Under pressure I keep telling myself, I've birdied and parred this hole before, there's no particular reason why, in this situation, I can't again.

I just kept telling myself, I know you can do it, so don't be an idiot.

The 18th is about 330 yards long. There is a series of bunkers on the left, and if you hit any of them you're dead. All the bunkers in an Open are raked with a wide-tooth rake which produces nasty ridges. It's rare when you can get a good enough lie to play a decent iron shot; you can get out, but that's about all.

I'd been having good luck with my old reliable, the No. 4 wood, up to that point. If I hit a good shot with it, I figured it would leave me a No. 9 iron or a wedge to the green.

I elected to stick with the club I had confidence in, the No. 4 wood, and I hit it exactly where I wanted it. Now I had a perfect lie on the left side of the fairway. This hole is a slight dog-leg, and my tee shot left me about a three-quarter wedge.

I hit one of my best wedges, which went right for the flag. For a moment I thought I had holed it for an eagle. But it rolled on past about eight or nine feet.

The green is in two plateaus. The right side is much higher. So when I hit the wedge the only thing I had in mind was to keep it down on the lower level where there is a reasonably flat surface. On the high side there was a quick-breaking putt.

Still, if you left the wedge short, there was a big yawning bunker right in front of the flag. Then you were out of luck and you'd have a hard time getting down in two for your par.

The answer was to be bold with the wedge to clear the bunker, but short of the cup, if possible, so that there would be an uphill putt to the cup.

I didn't hit the ball quite that fine. The wedge shot was good—but not perfect. As I said, it looked as if it was going to hole out, which would have been one of those "miracle" shots. However, instead I now had a slightly more difficult putt.

But I holed the ball for my birdie.

That gave me a 282 for the four rounds; one less than Demaret.

Meanwhile, of course, Boros was also trying to catch Jimmy. On 18th, he too had a birdie. But his second shot landed on the right side of the green and he didn't drop his putt. So he finished with a 284.

Meanwhile, Middlecoff was still out on the course. The first day he got 71, then took a 75 on the second round. At that point I tied for first with 138, and nine strokes in front of Cary.

However, on the third round he got hot with a 68 to put him only three back of Jimmy, and in a tie with Boros. It is mighty rare for a golfer to stay hot on both the third and the fourth round.

But Cary was in the process of putting together two of the greatest rounds in the history of the Open. On the 13th he learned that I was in and that he needed two birdies to tie me; three to win.

He picked up one of them on the 16th; parred the 17th. So he too came into the 18th needing a birdie to pull even.

He drove well and laid a wedge to the green; dropped a tough putt for his bird.

That meant he and I were all tied and had to go into a play-off, the results of which are in the record book.

When I went to Chicago a month or so later for the Tam O'Shanter Tournaments, I wasn't playing too well. As a matter of fact, I'd played pretty poorly in Baltimore the previous week.

I wanted to find out what was wrong with my swing, but there's quite a crowd of golfers at the Tam Tournaments, and it is almost impossible to practice during the pretourney qualifying rounds.

So I went into the first tournament, the Tam All-America, with little hope of doing anything more than sharpening up my game. Fortunately, by the final round I was playing much better and posted a 68.

Then, strangely enough, I slipped again in the opening round of the $50,000 "World." To be sure I shot a 72, but it was one of the luckiest 72's of my life. Things just broke right for me despite my poor play.

That night I practiced hard and I finally got my swing back—or at least I hoped I had. The next day I did better but at the halfway point I was still far down the ladder in fourteenth place.

Now I *had* to start gambling. I couldn't play conservative golf; I had to go all out for birdies whenever possible. The next round I played well and posted a 70.

Going into the final round, I was five strokes back of Sam Snead and four back of Al Balding. The night before the payoff round I sat down and figured out what I had to do.

In order to win, I calculated, I'd have to shoot around 65 or 66 and hope the leaders blew a few strokes to par. To shoot in the 60's means you must give it everything you've got; you can't hold back at all.

On the first nine I played some great golf and ran into some tough luck. On one hole, for example, my putt wound up on the lip of the cup and just wouldn't drop. But then on another hole I went for it, ignoring the fact that the pin was very close to the edge of the green, and sunk a 9-foot putt for an eagle 3 on a par 5.

By the time I got to the ninth tee I had hit a series of good shots and I felt confident that my swing wasn't going to come apart that day.

I had made two fine recovery shots and two or three birdie putts. Whenever I was in trouble, I was having remarkable success getting out.

On the ninth tee I was one under par. On this hole, however, I hit a very bad third shot short and to the left of the green. I had a poor lie there; it was muddy and wet where the ball landed. I hit my wedge too fat and left myself a tough putt, but luckily I got down in a par 5.

Looking back on it, I realize that with a bad lie I would have been better off playing more of a pitch-and-run to make sure I'd get all of the ball with the club face. That error in judgment cost me a chance to pick up another birdie.

The 10th hole is an easy par 5. You've got to get a bird here, you've got to, and that's all there is to it, I kept telling myself. Then a good drive and No. 4 wood put me on the green. My putt for an eagle was just short but I got down for a birdie 4.

Now I was two under par. At this point someone told me Gene Littler had hit one out of bounds on No. 6 to take a double-bogey six and I heard that the other fellows were having trouble too.

Now I realized that I might win if I could pick up a few more birdies in that final stretch. I almost got one on 11, but the ball just wouldn't drop. On 12 I left my shot about 40 feet from the cup and took two putts for a par. Result: two pars and one birdie.

On the next hole I hit a lousy drive, one of the few I had all day. The ball wound up in the rough with a very bad lie. I could chip it out on the fairway, which was about 20 feet away. But that would almost certainly mean settling for a bogey, and time was running out.

I was in the trees. The only opportunity to reach the green was to take a long iron or wood and try to keep the ball low enough to get past the trees, which were about 25 feet in front of me.

I was afraid I couldn't get a long iron out of that tough rough, so I elected to take my No. 4 wood and grip down on it. Well, it was one of those shots that came off just the way I hoped. The ball cleared, landed on the apron of the green, and I got down in two for a par 4.

Here my gamble had turned a 5 or maybe a 6 into a par 4. Now I had plenty of confidence and on the next hole I almost sank a tough 25-foot chip. I birdied 15 and got my par on 16.

Now I deliberately drove into the light rough on the left side of the fairway so that I could get a clear second shot at the 17th pin, which was placed on the far right-hand side. I decided not to gamble with a No. 9 iron, which I would have had to stretch. Instead I played a No. 8 with an easy three-quarter swing and wound up about nine feet short of the flag. Then my putt dropped for another birdie.

Now I had the makings of a 68, which would put me nine under par for the 72 holes and one stroke ahead of the field. It was up to them to catch me; they'd have to sweat out finding a birdie.

Up to this point my gambling had paid off. But on No. 18 a par 4 should hold that one-stroke lead. This is the famous hole where Lew Worsham holed out a long wedge a few years ago in one of the most spectacular shots in tournament history.

There are two great trees guarding the green. If you were

on the right with your tee shot, you had no chance for a birdie because the pin was set on the right side of the green and the trees blocked your shot.

The only way to get home was to drive out on the left, and I did. From there it is an exacting approach between the trees. Your ball might easily hit one of them and drop into the creek which runs in front of the green.

Furthermore, the green is really tough with that pin position. There's a big hump, and if you're short you've got a tough downhill putt. The best bet is to play it strong and go past the flag, or place it to the left, where you have a reasonably straight putt.

My No. 8 iron shot made the green all right, but now I had a 15-foot putt that went slightly downhill and then started up again. I putted a foot short, but tapped in for my par.

Balding had a chance to catch me with a bird on the final hole. He had a putt much like mine, only a little tougher, and he left it short. Snead had an extremely difficult putt from where his ball landed on the green and he didn't get it either.

So I wound up with the $50,000.

That was an instance where I gambled and it paid off, but I gambled only because I had to. Even so, I tried to pick the holes where I had my best chance of beating par.

If you are playing in a tough match and you reach the point where you've got to pick up strokes, you must gamble. The farther behind you are, the more chances you'll have to take.

On the other hand, if you are ahead you can, and should be, more careful in picking your when-to-gamble spots. A few years ago Billy Joe Patton had a chance to win the Masters as an amateur because he played three daring rounds and they paid off.

Unfortunately he played the same way on the final eighteen. A conservative final round would have cinched the title for him. But by nature he isn't a conservative player and, apparently, he felt he had to keep playing his regular style while he was "hot."

I've taken plenty of gambles myself when I had to, and sometimes they simply didn't come off. You just chalk those things up in the book and hope next time the odds will even up for you. Whenever you gamble you're going against the percentages.

In the long run, if you want to win you'll only gamble on the holes where your chances seem best and where you have the most confidence in your ability to produce under pressure.

31

Some Playing Pointers

I USUALLY TRY to play well within myself on all shots. But occasionally there are times when you've got to "let out" your drives for extra yardage.

Ordinarily I play with my grip just slightly down the shaft. To get an extra ten yards, I go to the end of the grip. I initiate a slightly larger turn to extend the arc of my swing and I increase my tempo both going back and coming down. The rhythm of my swing, however, remains the same.

Some players, to get extra yardage, bring the club head farther around so that the shaft is well below parallel on the backswing. But I find such a swing exposes my right elbow, and that can lead to trouble.

In general I'd say that most players would be better off relying on a somewhat speeded-up tempo for those extra yards.

One of the toughest problems for any golfer is playing a shot where you are not quite sure of the proper club. This becomes doubly difficult when you're under pressure to get your par or birdie.

If, for example, there's a choice between a light No. 5 iron and a firm No. 6, I urge you to pick the No. 6. That's because you've got a lot of nervous energy penned up at this point and as a result you'll be swinging faster than usual.

To play a finesse shot now would be almost suicide. You'd probably find yourself hitting a full shot and going right over the green.

Years ago Byron Nelson, one of the all-time greats, told me that when he got into a really tight spot, particularly on his drive, he always hit it as hard as he could, because that's what his souped-up energy called for.

I've followed his advice many times and it works for me.

But above all, let me stress this point: When you're under pressure, play the shot in which you have the most confidence. That's the best way to control the jitters.

In an earlier chapter I mentioned that I rarely watch another golfer drive for fear that his tempo may start creeping into my game. Unconsciously I begin to let out my swing to keep up with the longer hitters.

You should guard against watching another player on the fairway as well. One of the old pros gave me quite a lesson around 1950. We were playing Pebble Beach, and my drive was about three yards ahead of his.

My opponent then hit a No. 4 wood which landed on the green. This puzzled me. I looked at the distance and said to myself, it can't be that far away, can it? But, the more I looked, the more timid I became. So I took out my No. 2 iron and promptly belted it thirty yards over the green.

What I didn't know was that this pro could take a full swing with his No. 4 wood and then slow down his swing to a powder puff at impact.

So if you're going to be what we call a "bag-watcher," you've got to know the game your opponent plays. You not only have to know what he can do with a regular shot, but also what tricks he can play with a gripped-down, a punch, or a three-quarters shot—in fact all the finesse shots in his bag.

If you are matched with a golfer who has a simple, consistent game, and he shoots before you, you may gain something by noting the club he has used and the results he got with it. Perhaps you can apply that knowledge to your own problem.

Most times, however, you are better off playing your own game, following your own judgment of club and distance. If you make any mistakes, make sure they're your own; not an error you've picked up from another player.

32

Playing a Strange Course

GOLFERS AS A RULE play mostly on their home course. However, some like the variety of tackling as many new courses as they can. Golfers who play public courses often shift around from one to another. And even the member of a private club plays away from home now and then with the boss, a friend, or a customer.

At this point he may be confronted with the problem of playing a course he has never seen before. He usually doesn't have time to warm up or look around—he's got to go out cold and "discover" the course during his match.

Pros do a lot of traveling and are constantly faced with new courses. Every once in a while somebody asks me how I remember the details of a given layout. Well, take Tam O'Shanter in Chicago. I've played it a number of times over the years. And once I've played the 72 holes that make up most tournaments, I know a course and I'll remember it.

However, I can't always retain the details, particularly such things as where the pins are placed.

But each course has about four placements (a tip to remember) and they don't vary much.

However, if, as occasionally happens, I've arrived at a strange course just in time for a tournament with no advance practice rounds, I've got to learn about each hole as I go.

If it's a particularly tricky course, I'll hope to get a caddy who can tell me the layout: where the bunkers are; if there are any "blind" holes, and so forth.

Then, assuming I can get a pretty good look at each hole, I'll check the golf card for yardage, particularly the par 3's. It's relatively easy to judge distance if you're "tuned in" properly, and you must be on the pro circuit. However, distances on some holes are deceiving—and the score card is a help even to us.

If you are playing a course for the first time, I suggest you adopt a conservative game. For example, shoot for the center of all greens. Just try to hit the ball and keep it in play and don't get too ambitious.

When you aim for the center of the green, you're relying on your putting a little bit more than usual. But you are giving yourself a margin of error to the right and to the left for the shot that doesn't come off as true as you'd hoped.

Over a period of time playing that way will pay off, percentage-wise. You can't go for every pin that is tucked in the corner of a green.

Take a cut No. 3 iron, for example, where the pin is on the right. You'll have to aim a bit to the left because your ball is going to come in left-to-right provided you hit a slight fade.

If you make a particularly fine shot you're likely to wind up about three feet from the pin. However, you never can be quite positive how much cut you'll get.

But, by aiming for the center of the greens, you've left yourself the "safe" margin of error.

There is one other tip I'd like to give you. If you are playing another course in your same general area, you'll probably encounter similar conditions of sand, greens, fairway, and rough to that on your home course.

But if, for example, you go from the Midwest either to California or to Florida, you'll find a number of differences in wind conditions, putting greens, and so forth. Then the first round or so should be devoted to "feeling out" the course and adjusting your game to this new setup.

Also if you go from a public course to a private club, you'll soon find things much tougher. On public courses the fairways are wide; the rough is kept trimmed, and the sand traps are not difficult. A public-fee course has to deal in volume traffic, so they've deliberately lightened up the hazards to make play steady and relatively fast.

Playing a public course, then, you can afford to take more gambles, because the hazards (and hence the odds) are less of a problem. The converse applies when a golfer, used to public courses, plays on a well-run private course. Here he must be cautious because the hazards, comparatively speaking, are greater and tougher.

On any course which is new to me I generally try to size up the hazards to see how they affect my percentage game. If the hazards are well placed, I'll play conservatively; if they aren't too big a problem, I'll gamble more frequently.

The size of greens will vary from course to course. Usually the courses with bigger greens compensate by making them tougher. At the Augusta (Ga.) Masters, you've got to learn the greens by practice; they are among the trickiest in the world.

Here you'll often play an approach or even a long putt deliberately *away* from the cup in order to find a level surface for your tap-in. There isn't any "quick" way to beat a layout like that. You can only play your best the first time out and hope to pick up pointers for later rounds.

But the average "strange" course isn't very strange at all. The dog-legs may go a different direction; the water holes may vary; each course will be different in *detail*. Still, you'll find many holes similar to holes on your home course with which you are familiar. Once you spot that familiarity, you have your "home-course" confidence.

Nevertheless, use good judgment when you play away from home. Gamble only if you are *absolutely positive;* otherwise play conservatively. It'll pay off until you learn enough about the new course to gamble *intelligently*.

PART V

33

Taking Care of Your Equipment

Y OU CAN'T CUT a lawn with an unsharpened mower, or perform any other task adequately with poor equipment. Yet a great many golfers unnecessarily penalize themselves in this manner.

I am shocked at the number of amateurs who neglect the simplest detail of all: they play with dirty or scuffed-up balls and still expect, somehow, to shoot good golf.

I won't even practice with anything but clean golf balls. When I check in at night after a tournament, I dump all my practice balls into a bathtub with a detergent and a brush and scrub them up. It only takes a few minutes.

When I play I carry six golf balls. I use the first three on the front nine. If I make a birdie, I'll keep playing with that ball until I make a par. Then I switch to another one. I'm using a little psychology on myself; and perhaps I'm a wee bit superstitious as well.

At the end of nine holes, if any of those balls are chipped

or marred in any way, I discard all three and take out a fresh pack. Normally I'll use a half-dozen balls in eighteen holes. Then I toss them into my practice bag. Now I know the average golfer isn't likely to be that "extravagant." In my business, of course, it's not extravagance, but good common sense. Still, nobody should play with a scuffed-up ball. Every "dimple" is there for a purpose, and when a ball gets cut or damaged it isn't going to fly as true as an unmarked ball.

I don't think it's even smart to practice with bad balls. Remember that you are attempting to duplicate the shots you play on a regular round.

But the most inexcusable fault of all is a failure to keep your golf ball clean during a round. A spot of dirt can throw a drive or a putt way off line because it destroys the delicate balance that was built into the ball originally. I insist that my caddy keep my golf balls spotlessly clean. Whether you play with a caddy, ride a cart, or tote your own, I strongly recommend that you keep your ball free of damaging dirt by using washers frequently, and if possible carry a wet towel on your cart or in your bag.

I insist that my caddy use the towel to keep my grips and the face of my club heads as clean as you would your knife and fork. An unclean grip makes your hold of the club insecure.

An unclean club face will not strike the ball absolutely squarely and with spin. If you let the scoring marks on your irons get clogged with grass, their value is lost completely.

Most country clubs take care of your clubs for a modest fee.

A gentle detergent and a small piece of steel wool will remove mild stains and discolorations. But be careful not to destroy the scoring marks (the indentations) on the front of the blade.

If the marks are almost gone, I take a three-quarter file and carefully replace them. However, pros must be especially careful about this because we have a strong rule about scoring marks.

When the shafts become pitted, there is little you yourself can do. You had better send your clubs back to the factory and have the shafts replated.

I use furniture wax or polish to keep my woods looking right. I also check the face. If the lacquer is starting to wear, I revarnish or relacquer it. I always keep a good coat of wax on my woods to keep any moisture from creeping in. A good cleaner or wax, such as you use on your car, is satisfactory.

You should also check the bottom of your woods. Sometimes because of swelling of the wood and other causes, the screws holding the plate may be loosened.

If you take the plate off when dirt and grass have worked their way underneath, be careful. The plate is very pliable. But anyone who is reasonably handy with tools can do the job. Be sure to check each screw carefully. Each is a different size, and you must replace them in exactly the same order.

I use all-weather grips. When they get greasy, I wash them with a cleaner and a good stiff brush. If you have leather grips, either a cleaner or soap will remove the oiliness and restore the tackiness.

When it comes to the more complicated jobs—fixing a cracked head, replacing grips and windings, etc.—you should go to your pro or golf-repair shop. Your pro is an expert at this work and will do it much faster and better than you could yourself.

He is also the man to see if you are buying your first set of clubs, or if the time has come to replace that old set. It is his business to fit you to the right set of clubs to suit your game.

My own golf clubs are the new glass-shafted clubs made by Golfcraft. I find they give me better "feel." And because of the glass shaft they are torsion-free at ball impact.

I also use a D-1 swingweight, which is light but right for me. With my style of play, I use clubs which are proportionately an inch longer than standard.

These are my own preferences. But there is a golf club made that is exactly right for you, your game, and your swing. Your pro will help you find it.

He's also a good adviser on when to switch clubs. You can play with one set a lifetime if you care for them properly. But if your game is improving steadily, you may find that your stronger swing no longer fits your old clubs.

You should also care for the rest of your golfing equipment. Check your spikes occasionally and if they are worn down, replace them. This is a simple job for you or for your pro.

Wear the right kind of clothing. A binding shirt, ill-fitting socks or shoes, anything which interferes with your concentration is going to harm your game.

Every pro carries along rain protection in case it storms when he is in the middle of a match and can't quit. A rain jacket is a "must" for a pro golfer. All of us also carry an umbrella to keep our grips dry.

I don't advise using sun glasses. They seem to distort your view of your golfing problem. But a hat or cap to shade your eyes in bright sun is very helpful.

The other item—golf gloves—I'll discuss in the next chapter.

34

Off-Season Golf Tips

IF YOU LIVE in a warm climate, you can play golf almost the whole year around. Even in the North some people enjoy "polar-bear" golf in the dead of winter with red balls in the snow. But for a large part of the golfing world, winter means a layoff from the game. That is, a layoff from competitive golf.

But most large cities have indoor driving ranges where you can keep your game in shape. And even without this aid, you don't have to stop entirely.

As a matter of fact, those winter months actually can be helpful. In the preceding chapters I have outlined a number of lessons that can be followed indoors. You can work on your tap-putt stroke, as I suggested, using a chair leg or wall to train that short, decisive swing.

Most ceilings aren't high enough for you to practice a full swing indoors, but you can work on short chip shots. A small piece of cheap carpeting will safeguard your regular rug and quiet any objection from your wife that you are turning the living room into a driving range.

Another stroke which takes a lot of practice (and you'll have plenty of time for it in the winter) is the punch shot. It is done, as you well know, with a short backswing and a low follow-through. Only constant practice will train your hands to keep ahead of the club head. You can get the proper feel indoors. And you can also learn how to execute the cut shot with a short half swing.

The punch and cut shots are vital to the good golfer. You can profitably spend those winter months improving your golf game by working with a short iron on these two "finesse" shots.

This winter practice can prove a real short cut for the higher-handicap golfer. If you'll check your grip, stance, chips, and putting over the winter season and practice regularly you'll find you're at least a month ahead of schedule when you take the clubs out in the spring.

If you have a heavy jacket that doesn't restrict your shoulders and upper body, you can go outdoors any day in the year and work with my favorite practice tool, the weighted club. Even with heavy gloves on, you'll be getting the "feel" of the right golf swing.

The weighted club limbers up the right muscles and helps, as nothing else can, to develop a rhythm and timing to your swing. It also has the weight to warm you up on those cold winter days with a little healthful exercise.

Now, despite this advice, I know that many golfers will park their clubs in the garage or basement when the last day of Indian summer passes and will wait for spring to take up golf again.

If you belong to this group, please leave one club, preferably your putter, somewhere upstairs where you will occasionally pick it up and handle it, if nothing else. You may even be tempted to practice with it after a time.

Be sure, however, that the rest of the clubs are put away properly. Don't subject them either to excessive moisture or to excessive heat; either will damage them.

It isn't a bad idea to put a protective extra coating of wax on your woods and perhaps a light layer of grease on the shafts and the blades of your irons. Also, be sure you put your clubs away clean. The preceding chapter gave you tips on how to do this.

When I was an amateur player in New York State, I had to face this winter layoff, so I know something about it. Today, of course, I'm following the sun on the circuit.

Even so, I do have periodic layoffs. These serve to remind me that every spring many golfers have the problem of getting back into the groove.

My hands are about normal size, and I don't do anything in particular to keep them strong. A practice club and fingering the grips of other clubs scattered around the house usually fill the bill for any short layoff. I also use the weighted club if I've been away from the game for a longer time and must get my hands, and my swing, back into shape in a hurry.

When I start practicing seriously I work for a while without gloves. Then after a while I wear one to avoid blisters. There is nothing worse than trying to play with sore hands; as a matter of fact it is almost impossible to do so.

I use a full-fingered left-hand glove. I'll wear it until my hands get toughened up. Then I think I get a better feel of the shaft and my grip seems more consistent without a glove.

However, I use one sometimes in hot weather because my hands have a tendency to become moist, making my grip less secure.

Some golfers like a half-glove with the palm covered and the fingers exposed. If that suits them, okay. I happen to use a full-fingered glove because it seems to work better for me.

Whether you wear a golf glove or not is a matter of individual taste. If you are a once-in-a-while golfer, your hands never toughen up. Then I'm sure a left-hand glove is a help.

When you go out to the course that first bright spring day, *take it easy.* I think you ought to carry along your bag of practice balls (this should be standard equipment for every golfer) and warm up on the practice tee. If you play at a public course, take advantage of your local driving range.

Don't try to hit a lot of golf balls that first day. Stop as soon as you feel tired.

Then when you go out to play a round, quit the minute you feel like quitting. It doesn't matter whether you stop after five holes, nine holes, or when. Just don't overdo.

Too many people come out of moth balls and work so hard the first day that their hands are full of blisters. They try to make up for four or five months of idleness in one day.

The only way to start golf again and keep it *fun* (which it should be) is to begin gradually. *Play* yourself back into your game.

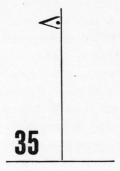

35

A Final Word

THIS BOOK represents everything I have learned from the world's best golfers, every hard knock I've had along the tournament trail, everything I could personally tell you about the game if I sat on your clubhouse veranda and chatted with you personally.

I have tried to avoid "selling" you on any pet theories of mine. Everything I have told you is tournament-tested and has been carefully checked with golfers of all shades of ability and experience.

I hope it has proved of value to you and your golf game.

I had a special reason for writing this book. Golf has been good to me.

Yes, this game has been good to me, and I hope this book will make golf more enjoyable and happier for you as well.